WHO DO YOU SAY THAT I AM

DISCOVERING YOUR GLORIOUS IDENTITY IN CHRIST

ROBBY ATWOOD

FOREWORD BY PHIL WYNN

WHO DO YOU SAY THAT I AM
Discovering Your Glorious Identity in Christ

Copyright © 2019 by Robby Atwood
All rights reserved. This book or any portion thereof may not be reproduced or used in any manner whatsoever without the express written permission of the publisher except for the use of brief quotations in a book review.

Printed in the United States of America ISBN 978-0-578-58609-0

Scripture quotations taken from the following sources:
Scripture quotations marked TPT are from The Passion Translation®. Copyright © 2017, 2018 by Passion & Fire Ministries, Inc. Used by permission. All rights reserved. ThePassionTranslation.com.

The ESV® Bible (The Holy Bible, English Standard Version®) copyright 2001 by Crossway, a publishing ministry of Good News Publishers. ESV® Text Edition: 2011. The ESV® text has been reproduced in cooperation with and by permission Good News Publishers. Unauthorized reproduction of this publication is prohibited. All rights reserved.

Scripture quotations taken from the New American Standard Bible®, Copyright © 1960, 1962, 1963, 1968, 1971, 1972, 1973, 1975, 1977, 1995 by The Lockman Foundation Used by permission. (www.Lockman.org)

Scripture quotations marked (NLT) are taken from the Holy Bible, New Living Translation, copyright © 1996, 2004, 2007, by Tyndale House Foundation. Used by permission of Tyndale House Publishers, Inc., Carol Stream, Illinois 60188. All rights reserved.

Scripture taken from the New King James Version® (NKJV). Copyright © 1982 by Thomas Nelson, Inc. Used by permission. All rights reserved

The Holy Bible, New International Version®, NIV® Copyright © 1973, 1978, 1984, 2011 by Biblica,Inc.® Used by permission. All rights reserved worldwide.

Unless otherwise indicated, all Scripture quotations are taken from THE MESSAGE, copyright © 1993, 2002, 2018 by Eugene H. Peterson. Used by permission of NavPress. All rights reserved. Represented by Tyndale House Publishers, Inc.

DEDICATION

I dedicate this book to my beloved children, Luke and Olivia. You two make Dad so proud. I am constantly amazed by the Father's goodness, when I see you following in the ways of Jesus.

I know every time I come home, you are waiting to greet me with the simple but sincere question, "Hey dad, how was your day?" The way you love your mom and me is out of this world, and I can't imagine any better children than you. Although it's bittersweet watching you grow up, I am so proud to see Christ being formed in you.

Luke and Olivia, Daddy loves you!

CONTENTS

FOREWORD

CHAPTER 1... Introduction   1

CHAPTER 2... Time to Explore   7

CHAPTER 3... It Takes the Spirit   13

CHAPTER 4... What Did He Say?   21

CHAPTER 5... Made for Glory   33

CHAPTER 6... Made in His Image   45

CHAPTER 7... Finding what Already Exists   55

CHAPTER 8... God and Family   69

CHAPTER 9... Children of Inheritance   79

CHAPTER 10... Sons and Daughters Arising   95

CHAPTER 11... Sealed with Promise   105

CHAPTER 12... Conformity: The Father's Process   115

CHAPTER 13... Comparison: Identity's Nemesis   123

CHAPTER 14... Tearing Down Structures   137

CHAPTER 15... Seven Enemies of Destiny   147

CHAPTER 16... Cultivating our Identity   157

FOREWORD
by Phil Wynn

Writing the foreword to such a groundbreaking work as Who Do You Say That I Am is both a tremendous honor and a daunting task. An honor, because I know this book is going to open eyes, shift paradigms, and change lives. I have known Robby Atwood for many years now and honor is at the very core of our relationship. He is like a son to me. That is something I don't say flippantly, because I am lifelong friends with his incredible parents, who could not have done a more brilliant job of raising two sons. Daunting, because I so believe in this assignment. I know what it was birthed from and I know the weightiness that the Father has placed upon it. The message of this book is the message of the Father's heart for this hour – this cannot be overstated enough. It also brings with it a great challenge to awaken the reader's heart to the incredible journey they are about to embark upon. Here is an adventure, I boldly say, that should not be missed!

Robby and I are cut from the same cloth. His love for worship, prayer, and the prophetic are core qualities that we share. His heart for the raising up of the House of Prayer is something that my wife Melinda and I have given ourselves to for the last 30 years. But there is something more. Several years ago the Lord birthed in me an aspect of the Father's heart that has become the primary activity of my life – the raising up of "sons and daughters" that would far exceed my generation in every way. Just as Jesus, expressing the true heart of the Father said, *"the works that I do, greater works will you do"* so it is our desire to see this generation do more, see more, go farther, and reach higher than we could even imagine. In Robby and Misty and the group of young leaders they are raising up at One27 House of Prayer, I see this being fulfilled. God is revealing the mysteries of the Kingdom to these passionate, powerful worshipping warriors and this book is the fruit of that pursuit.

At the very foundation of this world shaking revolution is the cornerstone of "identity." I remember the night at the House of Prayer when the Holy Spirit spoke through me to Robby. He said that God was going to give Robby a life-changing revelation from Matthew 16. The Lord has been faithful to that Word! In the pages ahead you will see those truths unfold, and as Jesus said in Matthew 16:17, they are things not revealed by flesh and blood, but by the Father which is in Heaven. Jesus was revealing mysteries to His spiritual sons – opening up the power principle of discovering and living in your true identity.

In these days, the enemy has tried to make that miracle into a catchphrase and a cliché. Stay alert though, because Who do You Say That I Am will make you feel like you have stepped into that Kingdom moment of Matthew 16 – and it doesn't stop there! Robby is guiding the people of God on a whirlwind tour which travels across the landscape of Scripture, and ties together incredible revelations that are both amazing and yet easily applied in our daily life. I am excited to encourage you on this journey and hopeful that you will find among these pages the keys to unlock the Kingdom. Just as Jesus had hoped, the riches of this generation are far beyond what has come before!

1

INTRODUCTION

I remember one of the first times I went to the beach. It was such an amazing time getting to experience some of the things that many had told me about – beautiful water, crashing waves, and the sand beneath my feet. It was awesome! At the time, I wasn't playing golf but just a few months later, I decided to take it up as a side hobby. After my first trip to the driving range, I was hooked, and I thought to myself, "I should've been playing this sport the whole time." Golf soon became an obsession, and to this day, it is still my favorite sport.

The following year, our family returned to the same beach for our summer vacation. Although I was excited about spending time in the water and under the sun, I was even more excited about hitting a few of the many golf courses available at our vacation spot. I didn't waste any time, and had my dad drop me off at one of the grander golf courses – it was my early birthday present. As I finished the round, I remember thinking I wish I would've been playing the previous year. By not playing before, I felt that I had been cheated of a fuller experience, missing the very thing that many travel far and wide to enjoy. In short, the golf courses were all around me, yet because I had not developed an awareness of golf, I missed many of the opportunities that were right in front of me.

In the same way, we as believers can often fail to realize the glorious opportunity we have by living in union with Jesus. Because of an underdeveloped awareness of our identity and freedom in Christ, we can often stand on the ledge of greatness and lack understanding of what's available in Him. This happens many ways, but somehow throughout life, we are given unholy boundaries and limits that were never supposed to be there. We're fed religious and wrong ideas of what it means to follow Christ. Thus, we often settle for a spiritual status quo, never exploring the greatness of being a child of the living God. However, I have good news – our Father desires to bring us into overflowing life and abundant fullness! He is the God of more than enough.

> *"A thief has only one thing in mind - he wants to steal, kill, and destroy. But My desire is to give you everything in abundance, more than you expect - life in its fullness until you overflow!"* John 10:10 (TPT)

Notice Jesus didn't say He would give us just enough. Nor did He say we would have to live impoverished. No, He promised lavish riches and fullness of life. Whether or not we realize it, this is what we signed up for. The life of a believer is a world of freedom. Some imagine the Christian life is mostly about keeping a bunch of rules, but this is a lie. Rules are only healthy when they've taken a back seat to relationship. Some think the greater things are for the "greater people" or those who have it all together – as if these people actually exist. Friends, this is nonsense.

To the Father, all of His children are destined for greatness. Everyone in the family is invited to *"taste and see that the Lord is good."* It's in the covenant of being an heir with Abraham. Like Isaac, we are children of promise, a people set apart to do His works (see Genesis 12:3; 18:18; 22:18). Although greatness looks different from person to person, the eternal truth is, all who are in Christ have a trajectory of abundant life. This is His promise!

INTRODUCTION

"And you, dear brothers and sisters, are children of the promise, just like Isaac."
Galatians 4:28 (NLT)

MY MISSION FOR THIS BOOK

Part of my mission in writing this book is to equip the body and speak into the Father's purpose of raising up a mature people. I believe maturity is one of the highest aims of the Father. Many times in Scripture, Paul spoke into this reality (see Ephesians 4:13-15; Colossians 2:6-7; 1 Corinthians 14:20). He used the terminology, "in Christ" or "union with Christ," and although maturity manifests differently, it always includes the dynamic of the head and the body operating in unison – it is the crowning reality of redemption. Bill Johnson puts it best when he says, "The Lord is returning for a body who walks in direct proportion to her head." In other words, the Lord is returning for a fully developed body who's walking in unison with Him. It's not that we are called to be perfect, just prepared (see Revelation 19:7-9). He wants a bride whose movements are in accordance with her mind.

DREAMING OF UNITY

Back in 2015, I had a dream where I was standing on the side of Highway 27, a major road that runs through my home town of Somerset, Kentucky. As I stood there on the side of the road only feet away from the house of prayer where I minister, a woman on a motorcycle went flying by at a tremendously high speed. I was amazed at how fast she was going. All of the sudden, she lost control of the motorcycle and flew over the handlebars and onto the highway. I knew immediately that she was hurt badly. Her body laid there lifeless, and when I ran upon the scene of the accident, it was quite graphic. However, the worst part of the accident was, the woman's head was severed from her body.

I stood in shock with many emotions running through me and in my panic, I picked up the dismembered body and began praying. I noticed there were several wounds on her body, so I started by calling on the Lord, and then suddenly, the wounds began to close up and heal. Slowly but surely, faith was building in this dream. However, there was still one issue – the head was still separate from the shoulders. I asked myself, "What use is bodily healing if the head is disjointed?'" So, I began to pray for the head to be merged back onto the healed body. Suddenly, the flesh on the front part of her shoulders began to form together with the head, and then stopped – the fusion was only going so far. In my holy stubbornness though, I was unwilling to settle for a partial healing – I wanted to see full restoration of the head and body. So, under what seemed to be the leading of Holy Spirit, I started praying in tongues and within seconds the rest of the flesh on the neck began to merge with the shoulders. At this point, faith was exploding as we experienced a full restoration of head and body. Within seconds, the woman was fully alive and restored to her original condition. As you would expect, we began to rejoice and have a Holy Ghost party!

MATURITY: A BODY UNITED WITH THE HEAD

I tell you this dream to say the Lord, through the working of His sons and daughters is placing the head back onto the body. For too long, the church has been in a high-speed pace of busyness, thus losing control of her destiny in God. This sort of distraction has caused a dire disconnect to take place, where her vision has been skewed. Thus, the life of the body has been forfeited. In our human strength, we've tried to bring healing to the body; we've counseled and cried with one another, and even prayed that all the schemes of the enemy would flee. These

INTRODUCTION

things are good, however, just like in the dream, all that was needed to see full restoration was for the body to be reunited with the head.

I have good news – the Lord is fully committed to raising up a mature body. In response to His zealous commitment, there's an apostolic people arising who are taking authority over the chaos. In simple devotion to Christ, this company of sons and daughters are becoming the hands that bring the body back into alignment with the head, Christ Jesus. Truth is, the head and the body are already one, it's just that we need to actually believe and walk in the power of this reality. In light of this, there is a people alive in the earth today who are fostering maturity and fullness!

Maturity means being fully developed in the abundance of Christ. This is one of the reasons why the Lord dispersed various gifts and callings to the body – He wants a fully developed picture of Himself in the earth. He wasn't satisfied with a one-sided (Moses, the man on the mountain) picture of who He was. He wanted everyone to know Him and extend His will into the earth (see Exodus 19:6). He longed to be fully re-presented in the earth, and He still desires the same today. Paul says in Ephesians 4:13-14, *"These grace ministries will function until we all attain oneness in the faith, until we all experience the fullness of what it means to know the Son of God, and finally we become one perfect man with the full dimensions of spiritual maturity and fully developed in the abundance of Christ. And then our immaturity will end!"* (TPT)

Interestingly, the Lord needed a place to rest His head, so He raised up a body. He is now calling us as sons and daughters to step into the level of maturity and new covenant grace that He has so willingly supplied. In order to do this, we must *"expel the son of the slave woman"* and give way to the *"son of the free woman."* It's imperative that we allow freedom to run free. The slave mentality keeps us bound and childish, while the freedom of sonship brings us into wisdom and maturity (see Galatians 4:28-31). The Lord of Hosts is calling His people out of the enemy's deception and control by inviting us into the glorious freedom and abundance of following Christ. Jesus walked in His Father's abundance and as we abide in Him, we now have the opportunity to do the same.

This freedom, as vast as it is, includes exploring the amazing inheritance that He says we have. It doesn't require a flashy resume, just a willing heart to run free and on fire! It's time to fully develop in the abundance of Christ. I'm not talking about the "bigger boats and fancier coats" abundance. Rather, I'm talking about where we walk as Jesus walked – the kind of lifestyle that exhibits the beauty and power of Christ in the earth. Where we in this world manifest who He is in heaven. Who will dive deep to discover the treasures of following Christ?

2

TIME TO EXPLORE

One thing I love about living in the Kingdom is the amount of freedom we are given in exploring the depths of God. We get the liberty of exploring Him and it's quite exhilarating! Friends, with dimensions of God's nature and character yet to be discovered, we have been appointed for greatness. Paul said it this way:

> *"And may you have the power to understand, as all God's people should, how wide, how long, how high, and how deep his love is. May you experience the love of Christ, though it is too great to understand fully. Then you will be made complete with all the fullness of life and power that comes from God. Now all glory to God, who is able, through his mighty power at work within us, to accomplish infinitely more than we might ask or think."* Ephesians 3:18-20 (NLT)

In this passage, apostle Paul refers to the four dimensions of life in God – the width, length, height, and depth of Jesus' love. Just as we have four seasons to live through, four directions to move – so now in Christ, we have four eternal spaces to explore. In other words, the Lord has called us into wide-open spaces – lengths unimaginable, heights unfathomable, and depths unshakable. We're not in Kansas anymore! Friends, we've entered into a whole new realm of discovery.

EXPLORING THE SPACIOUS PLACE

To search something out is to explore for the sake of discovering what is already available and possibly hidden. Webster defines explore as, "To investigate, study, or analyze: look into" and "to travel over new territory for adventure or discovery."

It's interesting that the Hebrew word for salvation means "to bring into a spacious place." In Psalm 18, this sort of salvation is what David declared when the Lord rescued him from the hand of Saul the grip of the flesh. Once under the mad rule of a jealous king, the Lord plucked him from the enemy. Ultimately, this is what happens to us when we receive Jesus as our Lord and Savior – we are taken from the suffocating clutches of the enemy and are placed in the embrace of the Lord. This type of transaction brings us into a whole new world of exploration.

> *"He brought me into a spacious place; He rescued me because He delighted in me."* Psalm 18:19 (NASB)

To be brought into a spacious place means that we have been upgraded to a whole new world of discovery. As such, we are now exploring the landscape of the glorious and risen Christ. He is our promised land. We find ourselves in a vast ocean of the greatness of God, a much broader place than we could've ever imagined. As we surrender to His leading, our eyes are constantly being enlightened and our minds are daily being renewed, to see the open freedom we have in Christ. This is the type of life that one could only imagine. Better yet, this is the life that only He could imagine. Paul said it like this:

> *"Things which eye has not seen and ear has not heard, and which have not entered the heart of man, all that God has prepared for those who love Him."* 1 Corinthians 2:9 (NASB)

RESERVED FOR NOW

Many Christians think this verse refers only to "some sweet day by and by" when we all get to heaven. Ya know, when we finally receive our wings, a cloud, and a mansion in the corner of glory land. This idea reserves heaven for the other side of eternity, being out of reach in this age. I understand why many would believe this, and growing up in church I thought the same. However, after years of my personal journey through the Word, I have to say that I don't support this idea. In my opinion, it's bad theology and is built upon the faulty bedrock of dispensationalism. This is one of the chief reasons we see a weak and powerless church. We've designated the mysterious and miraculous for the coming age, not the present one.

Let me make this clear up front – the *"Things which eye has not seen and ear has not heard"* passage is for now. We don't have to wait until we receive resurrected bodies to enter into this reality. Promise is enacted by faith, and the writer of Hebrews says, *"NOW faith is…*(Hebrews 11:1)."* In fact, if you read 1 Corinthians 2:9, you've got to read on to verse 10: *"For God has unveiled them and revealed them to us through the [Holy] Spirit; for the Spirit searches all things [diligently], even [sounding and measuring] the [profound] depths of God [the divine counsels and things far beyond human understanding]."* (AMP) Keep reading and you'll see Paul says, *"NOW we have received, not the spirit of the world, but the [Holy] Spirit who is from God, so that we may know and understand the [wonderful] things freely given to us by God"* (1 Corinthians 2:12 AMP).

The word 'prepared' (in 2:9) is hetoimazō meaning, "To make the necessary preparations, get everything ready." Interestingly, it is drawn from the oriental custom of sending servants ahead of kings, to level the roads and make them passable. This method of preparation allowed royalty to experience an enjoyable journey. If anything stood in the way, you can bet your bottom dollar the kings' servants were going to do their best to remove it. Another translation of the word "prepare" means "To prepare a feast." David used this idea when he said, *"You prepare a table before me in the presence of my enemies"* (Psalm 23:5).

This signifies that the Holy Spirit, the greatest servant of all, ushers us into the depths, heights, lengths, and widths of God's eternal nature. He prepares a lavish table for us in the presence of impending accusation, and while the enemy rages around us, He takes the things hidden and reveals them to our hearts. As the great revealer of mysteries, He is determined to remove anything and everything that hinders you from walking out this promise. And the good news is, the Holy Spirit absolutely loves His job. He thoroughly enjoys leading the children of God into increasingly greater revelation. It is one of His supreme joys.

THIS IS GOD'S FAULT

Do you realize that this type of discovery and exploration in the knowledge of God was all His idea? This is why Paul said, *"Things which eye has not seen and ear has not heard, and which have not entered the heart (experience) of man, all that God (the great Dreamer) has prepared for those who love (and entwine themselves with) Him* (emphasis added from the author)." Only God could prepare something like this. It all originated in the heart and mind of God. Before the foundation of the world, the Godhead had this stupendous idea that man and God could and should dwell together in perfect unison.

To facilitate such a reality, He has given us the mind (thought patterns and perceptions) of Christ. The world of thought that Christ has, is now in our realm of thinking. In other words, we can think like God – in every situation, we have the upper mind. Paul goes on to say, *"For who has known the mind of the Lord, that he will instruct Him? But we have the mind of Christ* (1 Corinthians 2:16 NASB)." I like to think that we have been hardwired with heaven's processor. No longer do we have to wait for "some sweet day by and by" to explore the fullness of God. Friends, we can jump in right now! There are no excuses as to why we should live bored and boggled down – we have the mind of Christ. We have the ability to know the thoughts and kind intentions of our Father. This is a game changer!

OUR GREAT TOUR GUIDE

Jesus described Holy Spirit as the One who would lead us in our exploration. I like to think of Him as our great tour guide. In John's writings, Jesus says of Him, *"But when the truth-giving Spirit comes, He will unveil the reality of every truth within you. He won't speak His own message, but only what He hears from the Father, and He will reveal prophetically to you what is to come* (John 16:13 TPT)." The things He heard from the Father were now going to be unveiled to us, His beloved. By way of revelation, we would be able to receive the very things we (as mere men) couldn't receive before His ascension. And while revelation would unveil the mysteries, wisdom would help us to apply those mysteries. This is why Paul prayed for the spirit of wisdom and revelation to be imparted (see Ephesians 1:16-18).

As we read on past the *"Things which eye has not seen and ear has not heard"* of in 1 Corinthians 2:9, we encounter an increasingly powerful truth:

> *"For to us God revealed them through the Spirit; for the Spirit searches all things, even the depths of God. For who among men knows the thoughts of a man except the spirit of the man which is in him? Even so the thoughts of God no one knows except the Spirit of God. Now we have received, not the spirit of the world, but the Spirit who is from God, so that we may know the things freely given to us by God."* 1 Corinthians 2:10 (NASB)

Do you see that? God the Holy Spirit searches the depths of God the Father and God the Son and reveals the riches of Their union. Ushering us into the company of the Father and Son, He sits us on the front row and points our eyes to the center stage of their fellowship.

"We proclaim to you what we ourselves have actually seen and heard so that you may have fellowship with us. And our fellowship is with the Father and with his Son, Jesus Christ." 1 John 1:3 (NASB)

The Holy Spirit investigates the depths of God, faithfully laboring to bring us into new territory of the love of Christ. What is already hidden in Christ, the Spirit wants to make known to us. In fact, the greatest news of the gospel is that we get God – we gain full access to our Father in heaven! Consequently, one of our primary mandates in this (new covenant) age is to partner with the Holy Spirit, that we may discover the hidden treasures and depths of God. This is what we were made for. The book of Proverbs calls it our glory:

"God conceals the revelation of His word in the hiding place of His glory. But the honor of kings is revealed by how they thoroughly search out the deeper meaning of all that God says." Proverbs 25:2 (TPT)

Prayer: *Holy Spirit, I know that adventure awaits me. I ask that You would grant me boldness to jump in with both feet, getting lost in who You are and who I am in You. In Jesus' name. Amen!*

3

IT TAKES THE SPIRIT

One of the most liberating things we can realize is the fact that we don't have to lead our own journey with God. We are not responsible for taking the reins and making things happen. Rather, we have a fully capable Helper who, along the way, is searching out the depths of God and longs to serve us with astonishing wisdom and mind-blowing revelation. In other words, it takes God to know God. The One living on the inside of us leads us to the God among us, that we may demonstrate the God upon us. Simply said, God leads us to God.

GOODNESS REVEALED

I was riding on the lake one day, when I looked back and saw a rainbow in the waves splashing up from my boat. First I saw it over my right shoulder, then turned to see it over my left as well. I turned the boat to the right and to the left, yet the rainbow remained. No matter where I turned, it remained there the whole time. In that moment, the Lord broke in with some cool revelation. He immediately reminded me of Psalm 23, where David said, *"Surely goodness and mercy follow me all the days of my life."* Remembering that rainbows in Scripture were connected to His mercy and goodness, I realized He wanted to reveal a portion of His nature to me.

I knew this revelation was calling for deeper study and meditation, so as soon as I got home, I went straight to the online prophet (Google) and began to study rainbows. I soon found out that rainbows are actually a revealing of elements that are already in the atmosphere. When sunlight passes through rain drops, they separate and form various colors. We call them color rays. Depending on the angle of the sunlight hitting the rain drop, determines what colors we see.

The rainbow is a revelation of His mercy – it unveils the mystery that man is enveloped under the canopy of His goodness (see Genesis 9:13). As the water who is Holy Spirit appears, we then begin to see the sunlight of Jesus. The coming together of these two heavenly forces inevitably displays the mercy and goodness of our Father. The mercies are always there, and as David declares, they *"Follow me all the days of my life."* I can turn to the right or to the left, and the mercies of God stay true.

> *"The steadfast love of the Lord never ceases; His mercies never come to an end; they are new every morning; great is your faithfulness."* Lamentations 3:22 (ESV)

These same mercies follow us all the days of our lives. They are ferocious, pursuing us like a hunter pursuing his prey. In other words, mercy will have what it's after. To take it a step further, although the mercies are already there, the Lord hides them to show us in due time. There may be days when we need an extra unveiling, and depending on the angle where we're standing, the colors are revealed. What is your angle? How are you viewing His mercies?

It takes all three of the Godhead to know God, and I love how the Godhead continually honors one another. God the Father points to the Son, who then points to the Holy Spirit, who then points to the Son, who then points to the Father…I think you get the point. The eternal cycle of honor between the Trinity rolls on. This is the form of fellowship that we are brought into as we say yes to Jesus and His leadership.

Our own personal zeal and discipline will never fully accomplish what He intends for us. It will most definitely help to partner our commitment with His, however, it is not the key. Our personal zeal is only a supplement to the key of leaning into the Holy Spirit. Jesus said in His famous Matthew 5 sermon, *"Blessed are the poor in spirit (your own strength)."* We are most happy and satisfied when we forfeit the provision of our own strength. Therefore, the primary responsibility of the Christian life is about learning to lean and depend on the Spirit. Those who do are the blessed (happy and satisfied) ones. If we're going to be strong, let us be strong unto surrender – looking to Holy Spirit, our great tour Guide.

"Who is this coming up from the wilderness leaning on her beloved." Song of Solomon 8:5 (NASB)

KNOWING GOD

As Jesus declared in John 17, eternal life is about knowing Him and increasing in the knowledge of God. It's not about escaping the fires of hell as much as it is about giving ourselves to the fiery love of God. One aspect of having eternal life for the purpose of knowing God is, we will spend eons and eons of time getting to know Him. We will continue to go from *"glory to glory,"* from one upgrade to another. Having this eternal mindset positions our hearts to receive His love. As such, purity of fellowship with Holy Spirit is an open door to see more of Christ (see Matthew 5:8).

"The Lord is my shepherd; I have all that I need. He lets me rest in green meadows; He leads me beside peaceful streams. He renews my strength. He guides me along right paths, bringing honor to his name." Psalm 23:1-3 (NLT)

As our great Shepherd and Leader, He stands with us and asks that we glance into the wide-open fields of freedom. He urges us to behold the mountains of His majesty, the valleys of His vastness, and the streams of His strength. Inviting us to roam the wide-open range of rolling green pastures, He places tools in our hands to explore, desiring that we discover the landscape of who He is and who we are in Him. He places in us the longing of prayer and communion, armed with the ministry of worship to grow in holy perspective, all while planting us *"with all the saints."* In other words, we have no lack in our God-pursuit. He has supplied us with more than enough to increase in the knowledge of God!

"I pray that you, being rooted and established in love, may have power, together with all the Lord's holy people, to grasp how wide and long and high and deep is the love of Christ, and to know this love that surpasses knowledge…" Ephesians 3:17-18 (NIV)

When Paul prayed that we (the church) would understand the love of Christ, he used the Greek word katalambanō meaning, "to lay hold of, seize, take possession of." In other words, his prayer was that we would be able to lay hold and take possession of the love of God – in the sense that we would discover the endless affection of Christ. When I think about possessing something, I'm reminded of the children of Israel and their quest for the promised land. Time and time again, the Lord would instruct Israel's leadership with encouraging words of conquest:

"See, I have placed the land before you; go in and possess the land which the Lord swore to give to your fathers, to Abraham, to Isaac, and to Jacob, to them and their descendants after them Deuteronomy 1:8 (NASB)."

It's almost like the Lord is saying, "I have placed My love before you and inside of you, now go get it. Explore and discover the endless depths, widths, lengths, and heights of my love – it's a wild ride!"

WE'RE GOING PLACES

About a year ago, almost every time that I went into a time of worship, the Lord would speak a specific phrase to my heart. It went on for several weeks. The phrase was, "In worship, we are going places, we are exploring wide – open spaces." When I would hear Him speak this phrase, I imagined a young child stretching out their arms, imagining they could fly. It's interesting that the most familiar posture of worship is the outstretched arms. In the same sense, I could see us (the church) flying through the air, as we explored the open space of His presence. Soon, the Lord would begin to speak to me about how, in the place of worship, we actually explore who Christ is.

As my friend Phil Wynn says, "We move at the speed of worship." One of the amazing dynamics of worship is, we are putting ourselves in the hands and embrace of the Father. As we gaze on Him, we are giving heaven permission to invade our lives with the love and power of God. This is why worship can't be confined to a service, but is to be expressed in a lifestyle. In other words, I don't just want to experience the speed of worship in a corporate gathering, but I want to explore it in all settings. May we move at the speed of worship!

If you were born before the year 2000, you're probably familiar with the phrase, "beam me up, Scotty." It was a phrase derived from the television series, Star Trek. Although "Scotty" was never part of the original phrase, "beam me up" was a command that Captain Kirk gave to Montgomery Scott when he wanted to be transported back to the Starship Enterprise. It was an action that would take him from one place to another. I imagine worship is somewhat like this, where we are transported from one realm to another.

Think about it, worship is the most practical way to intertwine our humanity with His divinity. It is the act of entwining heaven with earth. I find it interesting that when Jesus wanted us to bring heaven to earth, He first instructed us to worship. He said, *"Pray this way… Our Father in heaven, hallowed be Your name."* In other words, Jesus' first order of business was to get them looking upward so He could get them sending heaven downward. He wanted to transport them through worship, and before they could bring something to the earth, they would first have to go there. We can't take people to places we haven't been.

A FIELD FULL OF FREEDOM

In Matthew 7:13-14, Jesus refers to the narrow gate, later declaring that He is the only way to the Father (see John 14:6). As the perfect Lamb, Christ is proclaiming the singleness of His authority as the door (entryway) to His Dad's expansive and unending Kingdom. In other words, He is saying, "There is only one path in, and one door to enter this vast world of freedom. It is for freedom that I set you free, now come through this one way to experience the adventure that awaits you."

The narrow path isn't about the Father's list of rules on this side of salvation. Nor is it about walking the line of ridged or rigorous obedience, although obedience is required. Choosing the narrow way is about going through the only door – to explore the one and only adventure of freedom.

To make this clear, Jesus is our only way to enjoy fellowship with God. There aren't a plethora of doors to choose from – we don't have options when it comes to salvation. There is only one narrow (single) option. One gate, one way, that leads us to the Father. However, beloved, when we come through that narrow entryway of Jesus into the Kingdom, we step right into a vast world of freedom – one of encounter, discovery, and perpetual breakthrough. We step into a realm of "glory to glory."

The first time I went to Disney World, I encountered this scenario. When we pulled on to the property, there were signs pointing to the main entry gate. All signs led to the one entry that Walt and company had decided. As we approached closer to Magic Kingdom, all the people attending the park merged to one path, one narrow gate. The vast kingdom of fun and entertainment had one way in, but once we went through the main entrance, we stepped into Disney's kingdom.

> *"Then, as your spiritual strength increases, you will be empowered to discover what every holy one experiences – the great magnitude of the astonishing love of Christ in all its dimensions. How deeply intimate and far-reaching is His love! How enduring and inclusive it is! Endless love beyond measurement, beyond academic knowledge – this extravagant love pours into you until you are filled to overflowing with the fullness of God! Never doubt God's mighty power to work in you and accomplish all this. He will achieve infinitely more than your greatest request, your most unbelievable dream, and exceed your wildest imagination! He will outdo them all, for His miraculous power constantly energizes you!"* Ephesians 3:18-20 (TPT)

I love the miracle of Jesus turning the water into wine (see John 2:1-11). It reveals many layers of Jesus' eagerness to demonstrate the goodness of His Father. As His first miracle, I personally believe the Creator was sending a message to the onlookers, demonstrating that He would only get sweeter with time. With the inauguration of signs and wonders, He transformed the most basic necessity to declare that they'd seen nothing yet. Often times we can stand in the arena of love and fail to realize that His love is wanting to break out and blow our minds, transcending yesterday's understanding of who He is.

We often settle for the basic necessity of the gospel. We do our Sunday morning thing. We even throw in a devotional sometime throughout the week. If we're "radical" we'll actually pray for more than our meal. However, friends, He wants to erupt inside of us, with revelation of the dimensions of His love and goodness. When a billion years have passed, we will only have begun to step into the vast ocean of the greatness and beauty of

God. Let the adventure begin!

Pray this prayer with me: Jesus, I thank You that You came to reveal the ever-increasing goodness of God. You are eager to unveil the glory of who You are to me and who I am to You. As I move on into the journey of discovering more of You, I give you permission to blow my mind with the dimensions of Your nature. May the spirit of wisdom and revelation rest upon me, in Jesus' name!

4

WHAT DID HE SAY?

I want you to go on a trip with me to Matthew 16. To start off, I want to give you a little context. Two years prior to this setting (around 27 A.D.), Jesus had picked His disciples – from fisherman to tax collectors, Jesus chooses a wide array of ability and background to represent Him (see Matthew 4). From that time to 29 A.D, Christ spent much time with the twelve teaching them about the Kingdom, Himself, and the Father. In other words, they had pretty much been on an extended mission trip with the Lord of the harvest. After experiencing blind eyes being opened, the deaf hearing, and the lame walking, it was now time to do inventory of the Person of God. So, around A.D. 29, class began…

Many of you know the story in Matthew 16 – Jesus and his ministry team land in Caesarea Philippi and almost immediately He begins to pick their brains. For a moment, Christ pauses all ministry activity to do inventory of the knowledge of God. He first asks the disciples, *"Who do people say the Son of Man is?"* Responding with the ideas they had encountered on their two year mission trip, the young men answer, *"Some say John the Baptist; and others, Elijah; but still others, Jeremiah, or one of the prophets."* Interestingly, John represented the ministry of repentance, Elijah the ministry of fire, and Jeremiah that of weeping. Although Jesus embodied each of these ministry descriptions perfectly, He still longed to hear what they thought of Him.

So, in His wisdom, He doesn't stop there. He proceeds to ask them the paramount question, *"Who do you say that I am?"* Not fully satisfied, He goes from "Who do they say" to "Who do you say." His questionnaire soon moves from a public census to a personal one. Perhaps Jesus knew that if His closest friends could grasp the revelation of who He is, the public world around them would have a better chance of experiencing the same.

I love how Jesus used a rhetorical question to pull out the seed of revelation that dwelt inside of His friends. He knew what resided in each of His disciples, yet chose to pose a question that communicated the Fathers' affection. Even though the Son of God knew the answer, He wanted them to know who He was. Going beyond a general public consensus to one that revealed their own knowledge of Him, the Father really wanted to know their thoughts—not to shame, but to bring them into a greater awareness of who He is. This is the kindness of the Father, that He asks each one of us our views of Him. It doesn't change who He is, just who we are. Therefore, I believe this is the great question of the ages.

> *"What comes into our minds when we think about God is the most important thing about us. The history of mankind will probably show that no people has ever risen above its religion, and man's spiritual history will positively demonstrate that no religion has ever been greater than its idea of God. Worship is pure or base as the worshiper entertains high or low thoughts of God. For this reason the gravest question before the Church is always God Himself, and the most portentous fact about any man is not what he at a given time may say or do, but what he in his deep heart conceives God to be like. We tend by a secret law of the soul to move toward our mental image of God. This is true not only of the individual Christian, but of the company of Christians that composes the Church. Always the most revealing thing about the Church is her idea of God."* -A.W. Tozer (from 'Knowledge of the Holy')

I can only imagine the tension of this moment, as the disciples wondered who was going to speak up. What will they do with such a loaded question from the lips of the Word Himself? Is there a wrong or a right answer? What if they happen to answer incorrectly, and if they do, what will be the consequence? Many questions I'm sure swirled around in the young men's minds. Nevertheless, if any one is ever going to speak up, you can bet your bottom dollar that Peter is at the front of the line (see Acts 2; 15:7). So, in his eagerness to give voice to the prophetic moment, the young disciple declares, *"You are the Christ, the Son of the living God"* (Matthew 16:16 NASB).

Bingo, he hits the nail on the head! The passionate disciple had answered correctly, and of all the names Peter could've chosen in that solemn moment, he chooses the one that speaks loudest of Jesus' identity. Peter didn't answer, "You are the Lord of hosts, the mighty One of Israel" or "You are the redeemer of mankind." Although those names would've been correct, they wouldn't have been right for the moment. Instead, He answers with the prophetic revelation of Christ's Sonship, the prophetic word that was on the Father's heart for that moment. The reply of Jesus' Sonship is at the heart of the Person of Christ. We will discuss this topic of sonship later.

In this moment, the young disciple received divine revelation straight from the Fathers' heart. I could see Father leaning over the young disciples' ear and whispering the identity of His Son, as Jesus says *"Flesh and blood did not reveal this to you, but My Father who is in heaven."* In other words, Peter didn't hear this from a pulpit nor did he read this in a book, rather he heard straight from heaven – he had inside information.

CALLED INTO DESTINY

As Peter declares the Fathers' heart, Jesus (the Word Himself) then goes on to speak a word over him. The Father's voice through Peter releases the Son's word to Peter. There in that little area of Caesarea, the weight of

God's voice came crashing down, and this my friends, would change everything!

With Jesus' desire to give reward to those who hunger, He releases a revelation that would set Peter on a trajectory for the rest of his days. This moment of revelation would forever change his personal history, as well as the nations of the earth. It would yield a key for the opening of the gospel to the Gentiles. Oh, the power of revelation!

In the exchange of two identity revelations, Jesus literally unpacks Peter's identity and destiny right there on the spot. He doesn't take him to the latest and greatest Identity Conference nor does he recommend the latest book on destiny of the believer. He doesn't pull him to the side or call a special meeting but, right there on the spot and in front of all his friends and companions, Jesus makes a public announcement: *"You are favored and privileged Simeon, son of Jonah"* (Matthew 16:17 TPT).

I believe He does this for two specific reasons – fulfillment and accountability.

Fulfillment: Jesus was so eager to fulfill this word in Peter's life and as the Creator spoke, it was now official and waiting to be fulfilled. Isaiah declares that every time He speaks, the word will be fulfilled and returned to Him with fruit: *"so is my word that goes out from my mouth: it will not return to me empty, but will accomplish what I desire and achieve the purpose for which I sent it"* (Isaiah 55:11 NIV).

Accountability: He wanted Peter's eternal destiny to be heard by others, so the truth of his destiny was in the air. This would allow his ministry partners to keep him accountable for the word.

Keep in mind that true biblical accountability isn't just about keeping friends out of the mud, nor is it only about having to answer for an area of weakness. I know there is a place for checking in with friends concerning our shortcomings, but I personally believe that healthy Kingdom accountability is mostly about calling one another into greatness. We see this in the life of Abraham, when God called him great, as the fathering host for the nations of the earth. Therefore, accountability is about giving an account for our God-ability, not our human disability. Paul Manwarring says it this way:

> *"Accountability isn't making sure someone doesn't smoke. It's actually helping to make sure they are on fire."*

Healthy accountability encourages and challenges the call of greatness on our lives. If one veers off into compromise, the other is there to remind them they're better than the mess they choose. Therefore, as we understand our high calling in Christ, we will begin to call those around us into it. Paul pleaded with the church of Ephesians to *"Walk holy, in a way that is suitable to your high rank, given to you in your divine calling"* (Ephesians 4:1 TPT). In other words, we are to walk in a manner that coincides with our kingly identity.

> *"Law says you have to act a certain way to obtain something. Grace says you have obtained something, now start acting like it."* (from "Prayer the Great Journey")

God speaks over us that which we do not see in the natural. Just like He did to Peter, He addresses us by calling out our eternal destiny. Many times Jesus had every right to roast His disciples; He could've fired James and John when they insisted on calling down fire to destroy a people group – they were practically operating in a spirit of death. Instead, Jesus directs their "thunderous" zeal with a firm rebuke and later we see that they were of the top three disciples. Technically, they ended up being Jesus' senior leadership team.

Many times, Jesus saw their misguided passions and personal ambition and sought to guide it with His eternal wisdom. Time and time again, He chose to peer beyond the temporal and see who they were to the Father.

Speaking only what the Father says, Jesus speaks to us as sons and daughters. As His beloved, He speaks kindly and boldly to us. He doesn't just call us out of things, He calls us into one thing, our upward calling in Christ. The old saying goes like this – "My teacher thought I was smarter than I was, so I was."

When Peter stepped into this revelation, I can imagine it changed his entire vocabulary and ultimately, his mindset. Although Peter went through some times of testing for his identity to set in, we see the change manifest in his writings:

"You ARE a CHOSEN RACE, a ROYAL PRIESTHOOD, a HOLY NATION, a PEOPLE FOR GOD'S OWN POSSESSION." 1 Peter 2:9 (NASB)

A few verses earlier in 2:5, he declared we *"are being built up to be a royal priesthood."* He went from saying *"You are being…"* to *"You are…"* Peter understood the eternal destiny of the beloved was to be a royal priesthood, but when he said "You are being built up," he was alluding to the process of being transformed. The "being built" to us is an "already built" to heaven. Therefore, the Holy Spirit works from the end. He labors to manifest in us what is already a reality to the Father. God calls us from the eternal, not the immediate. Our divine Helper labors from the finished work.

HIS VOICE DEFINES US

Can you just imagine receiving a word like Peter did, on that day in Caesarea Philippi? I mean, what do you do when the living Word prophesies over your life? How do you respond when the Rock of the ages calls you into a realm of leadership that would forever change the course of human history? We're not talking about a general "God loves you" word, although those are still great. This isn't a feel-good Sunday morning message. Friends, we're talking about a revelation received straight from the throne room that would be a bedrock for the church to launch and be sustained. In addition to that, can you imagine the resistance that followed?

I'm sure the response of the other disciples was interesting. How would you respond when your friend receives the word of a lifetime, right in front of you? Can you imagine the disciples, in their human frailty, trying to cope with one of Jesus' favorites receiving this kind of prophetic word? Never does scripture tell us that the other disciples applauded or cheered Peter on. I'm sure there was some of that, but I also understand what it could've been like, especially since they were not yet filled with the Spirit. As I think into the narrative, I can't help but think there could've been some jealousy stirring. The enemy is always trying to stir up envy and contention between brothers and ministry partners.

I am in no way trying to say that the disciples were contentious. Rather, I am trying to pull us into the narrative to see some of the various dynamics that could've taken place. After Jesus released this weighty word, I can almost guarantee that all of hell came after the young disciple, to try to steal the word that had been planted in his heart. Isn't that what the enemy does?

> *"When anyone hears the word of the kingdom, and does not understand it, then the wicked one comes and snatches away what was sown in his heart. This is he who received seed by the wayside."* Matthew 13:19 (**NKJV**)

We know that Peter went through some intense testing. The pressure of being Jesus' friend was too much to handle at times (see John 18:13-27). Still yet, in the midst of the swirl that would surround Peter, Jesus' voice broke through. Greater than the voice of accusation and shame, it was the voice of restoration that called him back to who he was, even when he failed miserably. Christ became Peter's personal intercessor, as he was intent on his beloved disciple breaking through in his destiny. He didn't forget the word released over Peter at Caesarea, instead He called Peter to the completion of his destiny (see John 21).

> *"Simon, Simon, behold, Satan has demanded permission to sift you like wheat; but I have prayed for you, that your faith may not fail; and you, when once you have turned again, strengthen your brothers."* Luke 22:32 (NASB)

The truth of His word spoken over us from the beginning of time is what will sustain us. Seasons will change and people will come and go, but His Word will never change (see Isaiah 40:8). There are times when I am feeling weak and just downright vulnerable to the enemy. It may be in seasons where the noise is deafening, as the demands on my life increase. It may simply be times where, with no apparent reason, I just struggle to access peace.

In these times, I have learned to revisit past prophetic words that have been spoken over my life. I will break open my journals that I have used to record prophetic words and simply begin to read. Many times, I will go back several years to see what the Lord has spoken and where His faithfulness has been evident. I have to say, recalling the Lord's breakthrough in this way has been some of the most encouraging times I have experienced with Him. Where circumstances and noise can often block our awareness of His faithfulness, those recorded breakthroughs of God's voice bring my heart back into a sobering reminder of His goodness.

> *"I will also meditate on all Your work, and talk of Your deeds."* Psalm 77:12 (NKJV)

BEFORE MY MOTHER'S WOMB

We also see how the Lord's prophetic promise to Jeremiah awakened and encouraged his identity. In the midst of national chaos and rebellion, Yahweh tells the young prophet, *"Before I formed you in your mother's womb, I knew you"* (Jeremiah 1:5). In essence, the Lord was declaring that before the young prophet was in His hands, He was in His heart. Throughout their life and ministry, the Lord continued to drop nuggets of affirmation to both Isaiah and Jeremiah. Forming them in their mothers' wombs, He wanted to remind them that He knew every intimate detail of their lives. We think that all life begins in the womb, when actually it originates in God's heart.

In this swirl of revelation, the prophet Isaiah gets a revelation of God's care, saying, *"The Lord called me from the womb; from the body of my mother He named me"* (Isaiah 49:1). Later, he says, *"Can a woman forget her nursing child and have no compassion on the son of her womb? Even these may forget, but I will not forget you."* (Isaiah 49:15) These statements are quite intense and reveal God's heart for people.

What would cause God of the universe to express such terms of endearment? I personally believe the Lord was readying them to carry a heavy prophetic word to the nation, and in turn released words of affection to sustain them. He wanted them to overcome and desired that they minster from the well of His shared delight. God's tender affections toward us sustain us in times of testing.

> *"I am graven on the palms of His hands. I am never out of His mind. All my knowledge of Him depends on His sustained initiative in knowing me. I know Him, because He first knew me, and continues to know me. He knows me as a friend, One Who loves me; and there is no moment when His eye is off me, or His attention distracted from me, and no moment, therefore, when His care falters."* -J.J. Packer

Of this account, Charles Spurgeon says:

> *"If you will think of those hands of which the Lord says, 'I have graven thee upon the palms of my hands,' you may rest assured that nothing can come from those hands but what infinite Wisdom directs, and infinite Love has ordained. Rejoice then, O Christian that God's love does not fail in the furnace, but is as hot as the furnace, and*

hotter still."

We were a word before we were a reality. This means that God had thoughts about us well before anyone else did. Before human history began, we were predestined as His. Long before anything ever was, God had a purpose for His creation. This is how God works… He works from the end.

CALLING INTO BEING

I love how Jesus, in the midst of human weakness, pulled Peter's eternal destiny onto the scene. Although Jesus could've taken the chance to reprimand him for his soon coming failures, He instead makes a future reality a present revelation. Jesus' leadership is so wise and good.

If it were us leading this conversation, it might've gone more like this: "Peter, I love Your revelation of Jesus as the Son of God. It shows your hunger for the things of the Spirit. However, after some consideration, the disciples and I have determined that you're just not ready for leadership at this point; I mean, you're quick to speak, slow to hear, and quite honestly I feel that you still have some things to work out in your life. The spirit of prophecy has revealed to me that you will in fact deny Jesus not just once, but many times. It seems to us that your zeal far surpasses your wisdom, and for that, we are asking that you take a sabbatical from ministry. During this time, we think it would be wise to go through some training in our upcoming internship. Might not be a bad idea to close your social media accounts and focus on seeking Jesus for a few months."

Although I'm sort of exaggerating, I do think there is a valuable lesson here, especially in how Jesus relates to His disciples. I believe we would be a little more cautious about the risk of inflating Peter's pride, and would be more likely to point out the flaws instead of pulling out his destiny.

However, I love how Jesus was able to rise above the obvious outer and speak to Peter's eternal destiny. Anyone can point out the flaws in people. That's easy and obvious. Where are the ones who will labor to see people and cities transformed unto greatness?

God the Father longs to take the future reality and make it a present revelation. He calls into being that which does not exist (see Romans 4:17). We see this throughout the Word of God. He addresses Moses as deliverer (see Exodus 3:12), calling a man who couldn't even deliver a speech, to deliver a people. Prior to being born, He declares John the Baptist, *"Great before the Lord"* (see Luke 1:13-17). In the same way, He calls us by our eternal identity, not our earthly ability.

Since He has all power to initiate and create, these prophetic words were released years and even decades before they ever manifested in the natural realm. God understands the value of seed and harvest, and He speaks the unseen things over us, to see them manifest as we submit to the working of the Holy Spirit. He is a God who defines the end from the beginning.

"…I am God, and there is no one like Me, declaring the end from the beginning, and from ancient times things which have not been done, saying My purpose will be established, and I will accomplish all My good pleasure." Isaiah 46:9-10 (NASB)

LABORING IN REST

Gods' plans are completed from a position of rest. For example, in Psalm 2, we see that the Lord rules the world from a seated position. David says, *"God sits in heaven and laughs."* He doesn't pace the halls of heaven franticly, nor does He rant on His Kingly throne. Instead, He rests! The governmental throne of justice and righteousness is occupied by a King at total rest and in full confidence. Revelation 4 says that God sits on a throne that stands. The Kingdom that knows no rest belongs to a Man who does.

Therefore, let us enjoy the ride. He knows us by name, and understands all the dynamics of walking out our destiny in Him. Well acquainted with our struggles as well as successes, He is personally praying for you. Christ has become your personal intercessor, laboring from the finished work that He completed while on earth. Let Him speak over you, lead you, and see His word complete in Your life.

Prayer: Father, I thank You for the Word spoken over my life. I will not forget Your works, but will meditate on them and make them my delight. I acknowledge that You are more eager for me to complete my destiny than I am, so I submit myself to Your leadership afresh today. I cast all my cares upon You, and run headlong into the mercies extended to me by the work of the cross. In Jesus' name!

5

MADE FOR GLORY

"Everyone who is called by My name, and whom I have created for My glory, whom I have formed, even whom I have made." Isaiah 43:7 (NASB)

I was in fourth grade and my family had just moved from the little town of Eubank to the big town of Somerset. (I say 'big town' because every change feels big when you're 9). Although I was a little nervous about the whole school change, I didn't waste time in getting involved – early on, I jumped right into the school basketball program. I went from wearing Bulldogs red to Mustang blue, and I don't think my Eubank comrades were too happy about it. Anyway, I remember it so vividly – it was one of my first games as a Pulaski County Mustang, and I wore that jersey proudly. I felt like a million bucks, knowing I had just arrived at the school and I was already actually getting to play. Talk about a kid's dream!

The game was a good one – a great welcome for me joining the team. Going down to the wire, with only seconds left on the clock, we huddled at mid court. I really don't think we had any strategy or the slightest idea what to do, other than just try to get open with the ball. After our pointless huddle, we inbounded the ball and started our play. I remember thinking something like, "I sure hope they don't pass it to me." I mean, this is big stuff – there were probably 20-30 people in the stands, and most of those were all proud parents and grandparents. I mean, you can't let a family member down.

As the ball got inbounded, it was thrown my way. I then realized, I have to catch it and take the shot. So, in my eagerness to get rid of the ball, I threw it up for what seemed like an eternity and the ball went through the hoop. Yes, ladies and gentlemen, I hit the game-winning shot. From the hardest place on the court, the baseline, I sunk the shot that would bring us the title. Actually it wasn't a title, just a regular game… (sorry, got a little excited about the flashback)!

As the shot exited the bottom of the net, I remember what could possibly be one of the most epic times of my life – the moment when everyone piled on top of me. Yes, players and parents alike ran up to me, congratulating me on the game-winner. I was waiting for them to pick me up and place me on their shoulders, but it didn't happen. Still, that my friends, was a glorious experience. I can still remember the rush of excitement that followed when I sank that shot. It was truly a moment of glory – one I will never forget.

I use this story to simply point out that each of us have an innate desire to experience glory (in the sense where we come alive), even if it's at a young age in a non-religious fashion. Sometimes it may come through the glory of winning a game or of winning a lost soul to Jesus. Maybe it's traveling the nations to minister to the poor, or arriving home after a long day at work to see your family. The point is, we were all created to experience glory. Although we can fall short by choosing things that are only imitations, the fact is, we were made to experience the glory of His goodness.

Glory is an expansive word, and can be thoroughly expounded on. It appears myriads of time throughout the Bible and often describes the nature of God. However, I believe in summary it is the fullness of God. In the

Hebrew, glory is "kabowd" meaning, "heaviness, honor, riches, abundance." You could say, it is the heaviness of God, and explains why sometimes God demonstrates Himself in a weighty presence. You may have experienced this before, where the air felt so tangibly thick with His nature.

In the Greek (NT), glory is the word "doxa" meaning, "splendor, brightness, magnificence, excellence, preeminence." It goes on to describe glory as "the kingly majesty which belongs to him as supreme ruler, majesty in the sense of the absolute perfection of deity." In short, it is the fullness of God; the very splendor and majesty of God. (from Equip Collection: 'Identity in Christ')

JOHN 17: A PRAYER FOR GLORY

I love John 17 and believe it is one of the most glorious chapters in the Bible, as it describes Jesus praying to the Father before His crucifixion. A few chapters prior, Jesus introduces His disciples to the Holy Spirit, calling Him the Comforter, Helper, and many other grand descriptions. John 14-16 contains the promise of the Holy Spirit, while John 17 is the prayer of the Holy Spirit. While Jesus speaks of Holy Spirit in three chapters, the Spirit prays through Jesus in one. In this chapter alone, by inspiration of the Holy Spirit, the Son locks eyes with His Father and cries out for glory:

"After saying all these things, Jesus looked up to heaven and said, Father, the hour has come. Glorify your Son so he can give glory back to you." **John 17:1 (NLT)**

In John's 26 verses, I have identified at least 7 realms of glory that Jesus prayed for His people to enter into. One of those is the glory of communion and fellowship – that which is central to our relationship with God. The prayer that Jesus prays in verse 24 is, in my opinion, the apex of all other prayers that Jesus declared. It encompasses fellowship and communion with the Lord. He says, *"Father, I desire that they also, whom You have given Me, be with Me where I am, so that they may see My glory which You have given Me, for you have loved Me before the foundation of the world* (17:24)."

What would the Son of man say and pray as He faced the completion of His work on the earth? What would be His last words…His closing prayer, so to speak? Christ would utter these words, *"Father, I desire…"*. Right there, He pours out His soul and (passionately) expresses His desire for us to walk in glory. Not only does desire drive Him into prayer, but also leads Him to the cross, bringing Him out of the grave. All of these events reveal to us the passionate heart of God.

Through the death of Jesus we see the love of God, while in the resurrection we behold the power of God. If God were to be guilty of one thing, it would be that He is overwhelmingly zealous with passionate love for His people. This is why His eyes are full of fire (see Revelation 1:14). The Father's burning desire for mankind was the driving force of His devotion – the fire in God's heart fueled the action of His death and resurrection.

His desire was that we "be with Him" where He is. With Him, not just in the same room, but with Him. I think sometimes we associate nearness with partnership when in fact, they are very different. I can be in the same room with someone, yet still be so disengaged. Being a partner with someone in no way means I have intimate fellowship with them. I can live a business-based relationship with my colleague, and never know the deep intimate desires of their heart. In the same way, we can easily view Jesus as our business partner, someone we are working for rather than a Friend we are working with. A slave works for their master, but a friend labors with them.

Jesus cried out for companionship, and a returning to the way it was supposed to be from the beginning. He envisioned a people who would walk in intimate fellowship with the heart of God, those who would hear and respond to His word. In Song of Songs, the Bridegroom-King declares over His bride, *"How satisfying to me, my equal, my bride* (see 4:9-10)."

My wife and I love going to the movies. It always makes for a good little getaway from the mundane. It would be absurd to walk into the theater and go our separate ways. She could sit on the top row and I could sit on the front, and we would still be in the vicinity of one another. However, that wouldn't be much of a date. Plus, it may even get me in a lot of trouble! Rather, it is my desire to walk alongside of her whenever we are on a date – not in front or behind her, but with her. I don't need to pull back and treat her as an acquaintance, rather I desire to close the gap between us. Same goes for the Lord and His desire to be near us. It is what He prayed and paid for.

WITH HIM WHERE HE IS

Back to John 17:24 wherein He said *"Father, I desire that they… be with Me where I am."* So, Jesus doesn't pray for a general reality, He asked for a specific returning to a specific place. He passionately declares, "Father, place them where I am." Identity not only hinges on who we are, but also where we are. Let me ask you, where is Jesus right now? Where is He currently residing? Many of you will answer that question with a confident knowing that at this moment, He is in heaven with the Father. The apostle Mark says it like this:

> *"So then, when the Lord Jesus had spoken to them, He was received up into heaven and sat down at the right hand of God."* Mark 16:19 (NASB)

The apostle Peter declares that Jesus is at the highest place of honor: *"Now Christ has gone to heaven. He is seated in the place of honor next to God, and all the angels and authorities and powers accept His authority"* (see 1 Peter 3:22). Let's break down the three powerful dynamics of this passage:

• Christ went to heaven, the place of absolute peace and glory. This signifies the *place of His reign.*

- Christ was seated, signifying full rest and peace with the Father. This signifies the *posture of His reign*.

- Christ was given full authority, all of the earth is under His rule. This signifies the *position of His reign*.

Let's recap: Christ the ascended One, went to heaven and was seated, and now rules over all creation. Now, as a practical exercise, I want you to enter your name where it says "Christ." For example: "Lord, I thank You that I sit alongside You in heaven. I am seated in heavenly places. When I first believed, I was given the same authority that Christ was given. I am in Christ, therefore the things that He has and does, I have and I do." Pray and declare that you would increase in the awareness of this reality.

Since Jesus prayed and paid the way for us to ascend with Him, this means the place He is, we are there also. This means that identity isn't just about who we are, but also **WHERE** we are. This is our new location – transported from the kingdom of darkness, into the Kingdom of the beloved Son.

> *"He raised us up with Christ the exalted One, and we ascended with Him into the glorious perfection and authority of the heavenly realm, for we are now co-seated as one with Christ."* Ephesians 2:6 (TPT)

When Christ died, we died with Him. As He came bursting forth out of the grave, we came with Him. What He did, we did with Him. Not because we were strong enough to take death's blow, but rather because we were too weak. Therefore He gathered us up and died the death that only He could, to give us the life that only He deserved. While I was still a sinner, Christ died for us. What a glorious gospel!

> *"I have been crucified with Christ and I no longer live, but Christ lives in me. The life I now live in the body, I live by faith in the Son of God, who loved me and gave himself for me."* Galatians 2:20 (NIV)

CREATED FOR HIS PLEASURE

It's an obvious fact that each of us follow pleasure and desire. Serving as a compass in our lives, these two emotions influence our decisions and determine how we steward our life. Therefore, it is key to understand pleasure and its working in our lives. Webster defines pleasure as, "desire, inclination." Another source defines it as "a feeling of happy satisfaction and enjoyment." In short, it is an inclined feeling of enjoyment. What we desire to follow, we usually will. I mean, no one in their right mind wants to follow pain or disappointment – we actually do our best to stay away from it. Instead, pleasure and desire work in tandem with our will, producing our walk.

Every human being was made with longing and desire. From the firsts of Eden and throughout the halls of history, we see mankind looking to fulfill the longings and desires of the heart. Bouncing from pleasure to pleasure, men and women's actions attest to the fact that we are driven by these endless emotions of longing and desire. It's not something we can push away or even repent of, they are just part of our human make up.

The enemy knows this well, and that explains why he works so hard to pollute pleasure. In his craftiness, he will take the most holy thing and pervert it with a misguided pleasure. The God-ordained pleasures wired in us at birth, he desires to misalign and bring unto destruction. In the spirit of John 10:10, for example, he takes education and fills it with atheistic thought patterns that battle the knowledge of God. He takes music and instills it with corrupt messages that lead whole generations into wrong paradigms. He works among family and community to provoke contention and strife. I think you get the point. If he can place our attention to worldly desires, he can draw us away from affection and complete devotion to Christ.

"God's delight in being God is not sung the way it should be, with wonder and passion, in the worship places of the word. And we are the poorer and weaker for it." -John Piper

It is the Father's good pleasure to give us the Kingdom. In Luke 12:32, Jesus says, *"Do not be afraid (filled with fear), little flock, for your Father (in heaven) has chosen gladly to give (bestow and lavish upon) you the Kingdom."* The Passion Translation says it this way, *"So don't ever be afraid, dearest friends! Your loving Father joyously gives you His Kingdom with all its promises!"*

As we covered earlier, the Kingdom of God resembles the qualities found in Eden. Interestingly, the word Eden actually means "pleasure." This means that man was formed and brought forth from the base of pleasure. In other words, the Godhead pleasantly and purposefully crafted us, all because they eagerly desired fellowship with us. It wasn't a duty for the Creator to fashion you, friends, it was His utmost desire and passion.

The same pleasure found in Eden is found in His presence. When He walks into our lives, the peace and glory found in the days before the fall suddenly appear in our lives. In essence, this is what the gospel is all about – bringing us back into the glory of face-to-face communion with our heavenly Father. He not only rent the veil to bring us into the Holy Place, but so that He could see us face to face. And, I have never heard His voice so clearly, as when I came face to face with Him.

"God, keep us near Your grace-fountain. And when You look down on us, may Your face beam with joy! Pause in His Presence." Psalm 67:1 (TPT)

PLEASURE IN THE FACE OF GOD

It is the face of God smiling on His people that distinguishes us from all other religions in the world. No other "gods" pursue their people with eyes of fire and a heart of passion. Therefore, the joy of God found in the face of Christ is a game-changer. This is why Moses called on the Lord to bless, keep, and cause the face of God to shine on His people. Let's look at the verse with added translation:

"The Lord make His face (presence) shine on (enlighten) you, and be gracious (grant favor) to you; The Lord lift up His countenance (presence) on you, and give you peace (supernatural empowerment)." Numbers 6:25-26 (NASB, emphasis added)

For those who put their faith in Jesus, God's face now shines on them. In fact, we see that 1,000 years before the work of Christ David had a revelation of this, writing in Psalm 16:11, *"You will make known to me the path of life; In Your presence is fullness of joy; In Your right hand there are pleasures forevermore."*

Interestingly, there is no Hebrew word for presence. When Biblical writers referred to God's presence, they used the word "face." In essence, David would've been saying, "In Your face is fullness of joy." This explains why David was a seeker of God's face, for it was the path of joy. In Psalm 27:8 the worshipping King knew that in order to find the joy of God, it was through interaction with the face of God. The nearness of God, therefore, releases the fragrance of joy (see Psalm 24:6; 27:4).

Moses was another Biblical patriarch who loved God's presence. In Exodus 33:11, we gain a glimpse of their face-to-face interaction: *"The Lord used to speak to Moses face to face (presence to presence), just as a man speaks to his friend."* Engaged with Yahweh, Moses declares his dependency upon the presence of God, saying, *"If Your presence (face) does not go with us (shine on us), do not lead us up from here. For how then can it be known that I have found favor in Your sight, I and Your people? Is it not by Your going with us, so that we, I and Your people, may be distinguished from all the other people who are upon the face of the earth?"* Exodus 33:15-16 (NASB, emphasis added)

Seeing the joy on God's face sustains our lives. Just like Moses cried out, it's the face of God that gives us hope for going out. If His pleasure and joy wasn't central in the gospel, it would be a dire tragedy. However, friends I have good news, God is smiling! Knowing that our Father in heaven is smiling on us is a glorious treasure to be discovered, one that will bring continual freedom to our hearts.

> *"Glory to God in the highest, and on earth peace (good will, God's desire and pleasure) among men with whom He is pleased."* Luke 2:14 (NASB)

Someone's countenance will often reveal what's going on in their heart, and while we can't read what the mind is thinking, we can often sense what the heart is feeling.

It was in an early morning prayer time that the Lord spoke to me about His eyes of fire in Revelation 1. Sitting in my usual section of the prayer room, He boldly declared, "If you think my eyes are on fire, you should see My heart." As I sat there undone, I could clearly see that the eyes of the Lord are only indicators of what's in His heart (see Matthew 6:22). His heart is on fire with love and devotion for us. No one can or will ever change that truth.

Out of this bright and burning love, He urges us to look into those eyes of fire, and burn with the same intensity. Just like John the Baptist in the wilderness, Holy Spirit is the voice of One (in our wilderness journey) crying out, *"Behold the Lamb of God."* He takes the face of the beloved Son and points Him to the eyes of our hearts. This is the beauty of worship and prayer, that we get to take time to gaze into His eyes, becoming more and more like Him. The fire that burns in His heart can burn in ours.

> *"You have ravished my heart and given me courage, my sister, my [promised] bride; You have ravished my heart and given me courage with a single glance of your eyes, with one jewel of your necklace."* Song of Solomon 4:9 (AMP)

HOPE OF GLORY

Hope. I love this attribute of God, for it can take a life wondering and set it worshipping. Without it, we would be lost – and we were. Amazingly, the Father knew that our own human frailty and shortcomings under the old covenant would be a roadblock to experiencing His glory, so He instilled His Spirit (of Christ) in us. Under the new covenant, Christ in us would be our hope for experiencing and walking out His glory.

> *"Living within you is the Christ who floods you with the expectation of glory! This mystery of Christ, embedded within us, becomes a heavenly treasure chest of hope filled with the riches of glory for His people, and God wants everyone to know it."* Colossians 1:27 (TPT)

Hope in the Greek is "elpis" meaning, "Expectation of good, joyful and confident expectation of eternal salvation." This type of earnest expectation is released when the Holy Spirit takes up residence in us. According to 2 Corinthians 1:22, He is given as our earnest and pledge: *"Who also sealed us and gave us the Spirit (of Christ) in our hearts as a pledge (earnest)."*

GLORY AND GOODNESS

When you look at scripture closely enough, you'll see there are word companions that often appear together – words like mercy and truth, justice and righteousness, grace and glory, etc. It's like they have a two-fold purpose. Of these companions in Scripture, I have to say my favorite is "grace and glory." The concept of these two words coming together is amazing.

The first appearance of grace and glory coming together is in Exodus 33, the setting where Moses is longing for a rich encounter with the living God. While in an intense prayer meeting with the God of glory, he cries out for God to show His glory.

> *Then Moses said, "I pray You, show me Your glory!" And He said, "I Myself will make all My goodness pass before you, and will proclaim the name of the Lord before you; and I will be gracious to whom I will be gracious, and will show compassion on whom I will show compassion."* Exodus 33:18-19 (NASB)

Did you see that? Moses asks for Gods glory and the Lord chooses to release His goodness. Instead of God releasing the glory of His face (manifest presence), He satisfies Moses with the goodness of His nature. I've heard this passage taught many times, and usually from the viewpoint that God was giving Moses a little teaser, or that He was holding something back. I want to submit something different.

Perhaps God wasn't holding something back, as much as He was releasing a specific facet of His glory. You see, I think when we experience His goodness, we are actually seeing His glory. The goodness of God is found in the glory of His presence. In other words, when we experience His goodness in the form of breakthrough and His works, we are actually seeing a specific aspect of His fullness. Therefore, if glory is the fullness of God, the nature of God's goodness is only one facet of that glory.

> *"For the Lord God is a sun and shield; the Lord will give grace and glory; no good thing will He withhold from those who walk uprightly."* Psalm 84:11 (NKJV)

Just as Moses was hidden in the cleft of the rock, so we are now hidden in Christ the Rock (see 1 Corinthians 10:4). Now tucked away in God with Christ, we behold the goodness of God, and day by day are displaying that goodness in the earth.

> *"For God, who said, "Let light shine out of darkness," made his light shine in our hearts to give us the light of the knowledge of God's glory displayed in the face of Christ."* 2 Corinthians 4:6 (NIV)

MADE IN HIS IMAGE

"For we are His workmanship, created in Christ Jesus for good works, which God prepared beforehand so that we would walk in them." Ephesians 2:10 (NASB)

When Paul calls us the "workmanship" of God, he uses the Greek word "poiema." It's where we get our word *poem*. The definition of poem is, "A piece of writing that partakes of the nature of both speech and song that is nearly always rhythmical, usually metaphorical, and often exhibits such formal elements as meter, rhyme, and stanzaic structure." Another definition is, "Something that arouses strong emotions because of its beauty."

Poetry is interesting to me because the author's heart is conveyed in only a few words. What the author imagines as a world of thought can often be spelled out in a few stanzas. They have a way of pulling you into the mind and heart of the writer, and what the writer envisions, he or she will do their best to convey through words. This is why poems are so powerful.

Beloved, we are His writings and divine poem – the written masterpiece of the Father. In light of this, I believe our lives speak of the same. The divine Author's heart is communicated many times through our lives, working through His redeemed poems, to express and articulate His desire to others. We may be placed in the marketplace as a consultant, in the arts as a creator, or in the government as an official. Whatever the case, we are His poem waiting to be read by men. Paul says, *"You yourselves are all the endorsement we need. Your very lives are a letter that anyone can read by just looking at you. Christ Himself wrote it—not with ink, but with God's living Spirit; not chiseled into stone, but carved into human lives—and we publish it."* 2 Corinthians 3:2-3 (Message)

"You are a work of art, not a piece of work." -Lou Engle

Poems are comprised of rhythm, tone, and repetition. These three elements cause the poem to flow, all while drawing the reader in. In light of this, I can't think of a better poem than Jesus – He was the express image of God, heaven's open-book. His heart was expressed through the poured-out life of His Son. He moved in such rhythm with the Father. He released the tone of His voice, and His repetition continued steadfast. Jesus was and is the divine poem of God.

"So Jesus said, "I speak to you timeless truth. I never act independently of the Father or do anything through my own initiative. I only do the works that I see the Father doing, for the Son does the same works as his Father." John 5:19 (TPT)

Although Jesus was fully God, He was also fully man. Heaven and earth came together in Christ, and while Jesus is the perfect representation of the Father, He is also the perfect representation of a renewed life in God. He shows us what it's like to walk in the Spirit, all while dwelling in the human frame.

Although Jesus experienced the pressures of a fallen humanity, His physical limitations had no influence on His spiritual reality. Interestingly, He never allowed the external circumstances to dictate the internal reality of being a Son who rejoiced in the heart of the Father.

Jesus replied, "Philip, I've been with you all this time and you still don't know who I am? How could you ask me to show you the Father, for anyone who has looked at me has seen the Father." John 14:9 (TPT)

PREDESTINED TO BE CONFORMED

Romans 8 gives us a little insight into our goal as a Christian. It's a chapter loaded with identity, and gives us terminology like "adoption, predestination, and sonship." In addition, it contains one of the saints' cornerstone passages, *"And we know that God causes all things to work together for good to those who love God, to those who are called according to His purpose* (Romans 8:28)." It's a classic in the body of Christ. However, many times we can neglect the fuller context of what Paul is communicating, and in my opinion, the most important part of the passage.

In verse 29, Paul goes on to say, *"For those whom He foreknew, He also predestined to become conformed to the image of His Son, so that He would be the firstborn among many brethren."* Now let's put these verses together as one thought: *"And we know that God causes all things to work together for good to those who love God, to those who are called according to His purpose. For those whom He foreknew, He also predestined to become conformed to the image of His Son, so that He would be the firstborn among many brethren."*

As one thought, these verses go together like a hand in a glove, and should never be separated. In other words, if you consider the *"all things… for the good…,"* you must also consider being conformed into the image of Christ. Therefore, the key for this passage is *"He also predestined to become conformed to the image of His Son…"* In other words, the ultimate plan of the Father is to be conformed. It's not to bring an awareness to our circumstances, but to the mission of our conformity. In essence, Paul is saying, "Hang in there, because you are being formed into something greater – you're being conformed into the image of Christ." Look at how the

Passion Translation puts it this way:

> *"So we are convinced that every detail of our lives is continually woven together to fit into God's perfect plan of bringing good into our lives, for we are His lovers who have been called to fulfill His designed purpose. For He knew all about us before we were born and He destined us from the beginning to share the likeness of His Son. This means the Son is the oldest among a vast family of brothers and sisters who will become just like Him."* Romans 8:28-29 (TPT)

The church has often used this verse to make it through tough situations or circumstances, believing that if we just hold on, good will come about – when we didn't even know what the "good" would be. Although there is substantial truth to that, it seems that there has been a glaze over the church's eyes, not knowing if the good would be a better job, bigger house, or an easier life. This vague, general idea (of our limited understanding of "good") has caused many to grow weary in the seasons of life, simply because there was no vision of the good.

Although we know that we should endure "all things," sometimes we miss the Father's intention of producing Christ in us. If you remember anything from reading this book, remember it is the Father's primary will to shape you into the image of Christ. You were made to look like Christ. Period! This is His goal and the good of the gospel. Understanding this kind intention of the Father is what gives us vision for living godly in this age.

As a bonus, pressing on through various trails and temptations becomes less rigorous as we understand this truth. Paul could endure many persecutions because he knew the Father's end goal was being more like Jesus. Therefore, I believe it is imperative that we see the good goal of Romans 8 – becoming more and more like Christ.

Our focus must be on the Person of Christ, not the problem or the circumstance.

RENEWED PERSPECTIVE

I believe the question we need to ask is not, "Will I make it through this circumstance?" Rather, it should sound more like, "What will I look like when I come through this circumstance?" Do you notice the shift of perspective in the latter question?

When we gain a vision for being conformed into the image and likeness of Christ, we begin to rejoice in the midst of various trials and temptations, knowing that it will serve to form Christ in and through us. We can stand in the midst of a trial and instead of rebuking devils, we can actually rejoice that Christ is being formed in us. In addition, we will cease trying to escape the wildernesses of life, and begin to rejoice that He holds it all together for the good of conforming me into the image of His beloved Son. This is the goal!

Studies show that people who go to the gym for the sake of not being fat and out of shape, are less motivated than those who actually envision a certain (and better) body type. Those who go through the routine of rigorously working out with a "negative motivation" respond differently than those who are motivated by that certain "positive" image. In fact, the study goes on to show the one who uses negative motivation is less likely to stick with it. I like to call this principle "working from the end."

> *"My fellow believers, when it seems as though you are facing nothing but difficulties see it as an invaluable opportunity to experience all the joy that you can! For you know that when your faith is tested it stirs up power within you to endure all things. And then as your endurance grows even stronger it will release perfection into every part of your being until there is nothing missing and nothing lacking."* James 1:2-4 (TPT)

This is one of the reasons why worship is so key to the believer. As we behold Him, we are not only giving Him the glory He is due, beloved, we are aligning ourselves with the end goal, who is Christ. So, if it's true that we become what we behold, then I am cashing in all my chips to become a lovesick worshipper. Self-help motivation is temporal and fragmented, but beholding the glory of this eternal and Living God, that's the key!

IT ALL BEGAN IN A GARDEN

The battle over mankind's identity all began in Eden, the place of complete beauty and perfection. In the beginning of our existence, Eden was the centralized location of God's presence and glory, where man and God dwelt together in unhindered fellowship. I personally believe the garden of Genesis 1 was heaven on earth, the place of man's interaction with the Divine. It was the hub of intimacy and authority with God. Not just as a place of perpetual worship, but also where man received divine instruction and empowerment to release the ways of God into the earth (see Genesis 1:28).

In the beginning, however, the rest of the earth was in need of Eden's reach to be extended. The light of God's presence wasn't yet in every place, so God gave Adam and Eve clear instructions to bring the garden reality to the outer places. In other words, God was saying, "Make this experience a reality out there." The Father wasn't satisfied with leaving the fellowship of heaven and earth just in one place, He wanted it to reach into every part of the earth. Can't you just see the goodness of God, how He longs to bring His presence into contact with all people in every place. In short, He passionately desires unhindered fellowship.

So, in His eagerness to partner with man and woman, God commissions Adam and Eve to *"Be fruitful and multiply* (Genesis 1:28)." He gives them the mandate of bringing the Eden (heavenly) reality to the ends of the earth. In other words, God commissioned Adam, "Here as in Eden." Sound familiar (see Matthew 6:10)? In this storyline, we see that He trusts His creation with extending His dominion, allowing man to rule the way he saw fit.

"The heavens belong to the Lord, but he has given the earth to all humanity." Psalm 115:16 (**NLT**)

THERE'S A CHANGE IN THE GARDEN

This commission was going really well, then all of the sudden, someone crept into that inhabited place with one goal – to deceive Adam and Eve, God's chosen elect. Satan knew he had to attack in Eden, for it was the headquarters of intimacy and dominion – the place where God and man dwelt together in unhindered fellowship. Therefore, if he wanted to hinder the mandate, he knew he had to disrupt the fellowship.

The enemy had no dominion or authority at this point, yet he desired to rob it from the ones who did, God's children. While the Lord was commissioning Adam and Eve in the garden, satan was deceiving them there. What lie would he use to bring man and woman into bondage? What perversion would he use to taint the waters of unhindered fellowship and hearing the voice of their Master? Let's take a look:

> *"Now the serpent was more crafty than any beast of the field which the Lord God had made. And he said to the woman, "Indeed, has God said, 'You shall not eat from any tree of the garden'? The woman said to the serpent, "From the fruit of the trees of the garden we may eat; but from the fruit of the tree which is in the middle of the garden, God has said, 'You shall not eat from it or touch it, or you will die.' The serpent said to the woman, "You surely will not die! For God knows that in the day you eat from it your eyes will be opened, and you will be like God, knowing good and evil. When the woman saw that the tree was good for food, and that it was a delight to the eyes, and that the tree was desirable to make one wise, she took from its fruit and ate; and she gave also to her husband with her, and he ate. Then the eyes of both of them were opened, and they knew that they were naked; and they sewed fig leaves together and made themselves loin coverings."* Genesis 3:1-7 (**NASB**)

Adam and Eve were shadows of all who would follow, showing that we are tempted and enticed in the same ways. Therefore, we have several lessons to learn here in this passage.

First of all, Eve entered into conversation with the serpent. Going outside of her God-ordained boundaries of communion with God, she entered into a world of conversation in which she was never called to attend. Therefore, let us understand we are never called to have conversation with the serpent, rather we are called to resist and cast him out. When we enter into dialogue with the devil, we forfeit and move outside the supreme calling of fellowship with God. Paul urged the church in this by saying, *"Submit therefore to God. Resist the devil and he will flee from you* (James 4:7)."

In one sense, he was urging the church to resist conversation with their enemy. The apostle uses the word anthistēmi, meaning "To withstand, to directly oppose." It denotes a forceful action, and in no way speaks of a passive one. When we treat the enemy with passive action, we give him a foothold. Weak resistance to temptation soon becomes a crack in the wall, and when that crack becomes larger, it makes resisting a more difficult task. Beloved, when temptation tries to break in and move you to disobedience, resist it immediately. Give the enemy no foothold.

> *From day one, He gave man a kingly identity, a royal job description. He didn't just say "sit back and watch Me rule." He gave us the mandate to do so. This is part of the mystery of the gospel, that God (infinite and perfect in nature) would choose weak and broken people like you and me to take care of what He designed. He is a God who trusts people. Amazing! So, when Adam and Eve sinned, they handed over the keys to the house. The eternal authority they had been given was forfeited in a single moment. The grave sin of Adam and Eve was not that they simply disobeyed God, but they actually changed masters. In their obedience to the serpent, the earth came under submission of a new leader. From that moment forward (before the cross), Satan had full reign over the earth. He became its ruler. In an attempt to retain his authority, Satan tempted Christ with things like, "I will give You all this domain and its glory;*

for it has been handed over to me, and I give it to whomever I wish. Therefore if You worship before me, it shall all be Yours" (Luke 4:6 NASB). *He could tempt Christ with the earth's domain and glory because it actually belonged to Him. In addition, Christ could be tempted because He was flesh. And this is the beauty of the gospel, that the Creator wrapped Himself in flesh to give His life into the hands of men and women, even into the realm of Satan's temptation. God required a man to redeem mankind and Jesus stepped up to the plate! He didn't stand back from the clinches of mankind, rather He threw Himself right in the middle of it. It was His divine choice. (from 'Prayer the Great Journey)*

Secondly, Adam and Eve believed the lies of the enemy and thus entertained the perception of darkness. They broke outside of the boundaries of Gods' commands and entered a world of thought where they were never called to tread. We must understand that we only empower the lie we believe.

BELIEF AND BEHAVIOR

Initially, the enemy doesn't work to get us to behave, but to first believe. He knows that if we agree and buy into his lies, we will inevitably bring our lives into alignment with them. In light of this, satan, in the wilderness testing, attempted to bring Jesus into alignment with his lies, telling the Son of God if He would only worship, the keys of authority would be given back to Him. In other words, the serpent stood face to face with the Son of God and offered the keys of dominion in exchange for worship. In a sense, satan was saying, "I've always wanted worship and you've always wanted dominion, so let's make this easy… I'll give you the keys if you give me the worship."

The wilderness showdown all came down to worship and submission, and if Jesus would've given in to the lies of the enemy, all hope would have been lost. However, Jesus in His divine wisdom understood one key reality:

worship is directly connected to authority and dominion. You will only walk in authority to the degree that you submit to authority, and you will extend authority in the place that you give your heart to.

Belief will always produce some sort of fruit. What Adam and Eve failed to realize was that they were already made in Gods image. Holding the keys of authority, Adam and Eve believed the lie that they could become like someone they were already like (see Genesis 1:27). They became ensnared when they failed to realize what they had.

Isn't it interesting that the enemy usually wars against our minds by convincing us that we must earn the things we already have in our possession. He will work overtime to convince us that we need to do more in order to be more.

Maybe instead of deliverance ministry, we need discovery ministry. What if we become supremely aware of what we had, instead of falsely convinced of what we don't. (from "Exploring Our Freedom in Christ")

He said to Eve, *"You surely will not die! For God knows that in the day you eat from it your eyes will be opened, and you will be like God, knowing good and evil* (Genesis 3:4-5)." You will be like God if you do… Sounds a lot like the enemy's voice, doesn't it?! He works to get us doing before being.

All Eve had to do was resist and change her direction of meditation. If she could've only turned the enemy away from her realm of thought and hearing, satan would have fled away from her. What was for us inherited sin nature, was once for Eve an entertained thought.

7

FINDING WHAT ALREADY EXISTS

Many times, my wife will send me to the store to get some supplies. Sometimes it's groceries but for those more dreaded times, she'll send me in for some "female items." (You husbands know what I'm talking about). These trips are often somewhat interesting…probably because I am like any other man, when I say that I struggle finding what she sends me in for.

Just lately, she sent me in for 3 items and it took me nearly 30 minutes. Yeah, when I came back to the car, I was frazzled to say the least. I mean, sending a man into a crowded grocery store to gather up hamburger meat, buns, and dessert – that's a recipe for a panic attack.

During this trip, I remember standing in the bakery, saying to myself, "Where in the heck do they put the hamburger buns?" I'm sure I paced that section for 5 minutes, looking for what had to be there. So, after my failed attempt to find this simple item, in my humiliation, I approached one of the employees and asked, "Sir, where are the hamburger buns?" Answering with a smirk on his face, he then pointed over my shoulder and said, "Right there!" Before I turned around, I knew what I was about to see…yes, the buns were literally right behind me. The very thing I had wandered aimlessly around trying to find, was right there within my reach. Like a whipped puppy, I hung my head, walked away, and got my bread.

I tell this story to say this: many times we fail to realize what is right in front of us and at our disposal. In the same sense, we can stand in the room of potential and ask for the things we already have. It would've been absurd for me to storm out of the store thinking that bread no longer existed. Can you imagine me returning to the car, telling my wife that bread has been taken out of the market? She would've looked at me and said, "Get back in there and get the bread… It's a grocery store, of course they have bread."

NO LACK IN THE FATHER'S HOUSE

The orphan mentality thinks there is lack when in fact, there is more than enough. When we are convinced there is a shortage, we start wrestling for promotion and attention. This is where we get into self-exaltation and pride, thinking we have to help the process of promotion. However, when we realize there is an endless supply of goodness and resource to go around, we rest and work from the abundance, not for it.

I have fallen into this lie of the enemy far too many times, believing that I had to get while the getting was good. Although I believe that the Lord sometimes works in seasons, He doesn't feed us from seasons. It's not like there is famine and feast time in His house. He's not at the end of the table teasing us with just enough, only to get us ready for a season of drought. Instead, He is a Father who lavishes His goodness on us in every season – we just need eyes to see His involvement in all seasons. Although our journey has ebbs and flows involved, truth is, the Lord is an ocean whose currents are steady yet moving. As we keep our eyes on Jesus, we are now walking on water, the ocean of His love.

AGREEMENT

The enemy's intention is always to get you in agreement with his lies. It may be through a subtle whisper or an obvious shout. Nonetheless, the moment we agree with him is the moment that strongholds form.

While in rigorous and intense study of end-time events, I once asked the Lord, "What are the end times about, what is all of the unfolding of events about in the last days?" Swirling in a world of opinions and information, I had to take a deep breath and get clarity on the issue.

He soon replied and said, "It's all about agreement." It hit me like a ton of bricks, as He went on to expound; just as man and woman were brought together, heaven and earth are coming together, the Spirit and the bride are merging in total agreement, so it shall be in the last days. In essence, He was saying that all of the unfolding of events is to move mankind into the posture of agreement with His heart and mind. He wants a body who thinks on things above, the head of Christ. If He can get a people in agreement with His heart, He can have a people empowered by His hand.

"I can't afford to have a thought in my mind that's not in His." -Bill Johnson

As I stated earlier, it all goes back to the garden of Eden. Everything that God is doing points back to when God dwelled with man in perfect harmony – where the reign and rule of God was with man on the earth. However, as grand as this sounds, there is still a process of seeing this played out in our lives, both individually and in the body. We can all agree that no one has arrived, and we, like Abraham, are still on a journey as we long to manifest this reality.

PRUNING IN THE PROCESS

I remember the first house my wife and I moved into. It was a little bitty 2 bedroom with a tiny office. We were so proud of it and at the time, we were just glad to be able to call a place our own. However, it was a repossession with some obvious "battle marks," and the ole place was in desperate need of upgrades and some major TLC.

One of the first things we did was deep clean, paint the inside, and plant some shrubs – it was only the beginning of the repairs. We did all of this with so much pride and dignity, and you would've thought we had just bought a mansion. Misty and I both put our hands to painting and cleaning, but we decided that I would be the one doing the landscaping. So off to work I went. I felt like I dug dirt and pulled weeds for days. However, after the strenuous labor of uprooting and planting new shrubs, I remember stepping back into our front lawn and staring at landscaping work that graced our new humble abode. I was amazed at how much it helped the looks of the house. I was pretty proud of my work.

Well, a few weeks went by and as the season started to change, I noticed the plants were starting to change as well. That new healthy look they once had was now diminishing. There was one plant in particular that looked like it had been sprayed with weed killer. I immediately freaked out, thinking I had done something wrong.

So in my panic, I called one of our "green thumb" family members for some advice, and she consoled me and let me know that everything was okay. Apparently, it was normal for this kind of plant to change color and lose some foliage. However, what she said next didn't make any sense. She instructed me to trim the plant down a few inches from the root. I hated to think of cutting down the nearly two feet long leaves all the way down to a near nub. I'm thinking, "Yeah I called the wrong person." But after some discussion, she assured me it was going to be the best thing. So, I did what she said.

Soon the winter season passed and spring came, and to my surprise the plant completely rejuvenated its color and size. In fact, it was healthier looking than before. During the following spring and summer season, the plant actually grew larger than it ever had. I continued to prune it every winter season and to my surprise, it continued to grow healthier and healthier. What I thought was an "injustice" to the plant (by pruning it down), was actually an act that would cause the plant to bear greater fruit in days ahead.

"I am the true Vine, and My Father is the vinedresser. Every branch in Me that does not bear fruit, He takes away; and every branch that continues to bear fruit, He [repeatedly] prunes, so that it will bear more fruit [even richer and finer fruit]." John 15:1-2 (AMP)

Notice that Jesus presents two categories of the Fathers' vine dressing:

1.) There are branches He takes away.

2.) There are branches He prunes.

To take away is to remove permanently for the sake of never returning, while pruning is to remove temporarily for the sake of returning with greater fruit. One branch He wants to banish while the other He wants to bear.

Pruning can either be one of the most offensive or the most encouraging things in our walk with the Father. This all depends on the lens we are looking through. When the process of pruning is viewed as punishment, it can seem painful, often leading to frustration. But when we see pruning as part of the promise (of being a child of God), we can learn to rejoice in the midst of it.

We can either view pruning through the lens of an orphan or a son. (I'm borrowing these terms from apostle Pauls' writings to the early church.) Let's look at the diverse difference:

- To the orphan, pruning is betrayal. With the orphan mentality, we find our identity in what we do. Therefore, when He prunes the things we do, we view it as cutting off who we are.

- To the son, pruning is promotion. When we view Him as a loving Father who is wholly committed to our destiny, pruning is part of removing anything that stands in the way of us receiving His love.

PRUNING FOR THE LONG-TERM

The Greek word for pruning is "kathairo" meaning "to cleanse." It also yields the meaning, "to prune trees and vines from useless shoots." Websters defines pruning as, "to trim (a tree, shrub, or bush) by cutting away dead or overgrown branches or stems, especially to increase fruitfulness and growth." In other words, you could say pruning is "removing any unwanted or useless branches for the sake of increase." It is the process of taking anything away that hinders growth, not just for the immediate, but also for the near and distant future. He knows us far better than we know ourselves and is committed to forming us into the image of His Son.

The Father wants us to live a fruitful and faithful life, bearing fruit not just for today, but for years and decades to come. As my friend Josh MacDonald says, "The Father wants us 80, unoffended, and growing in Him." As a Father who is so committed to the process, His vision for our lives is beyond the immediate and more into the eternal. He envisions sons and daughters who burn with passion for His name, into our 60's, 70's, and 80's. He will do whatever He needs to do in the present to ensure that we are steady later in life.

> *"For we are God's fellow workers [His servants working together]; you are God's cultivated field [His garden, His vineyard], God's building."* 2 Corinthians 3:9 (AMP)

Being God's garden, we must understand that pruning is part of the process. If you were to tell a florist or gardener that their foliage didn't need trimming, they would look at you like you were crazy. You could say something like, "If you love those plants, you will just let them grow on their own. Being the loving gardener you are, you should only do positive things to the plant that doesn't involve cutting off branches." I know that sounds absurd, but the point is – what you want to grow and flourish, you will need to prune. Trimming the plant doesn't make the gardener a bad person, but a good one.

In the same sense, pruning reveals the caring heart of the Father. When Jesus said He would never leave us nor forsake us in Hebrews 13:5, He was committing to us until the end. He was pledging an eternal commitment to our hearts, minds, bodies, and our spirits. In essence, He was saying, "Listen, I'm not the kind of God who only comes around when you ask me to. Rather, I'm a Father who loves to stay involved in every season of the soul. I'm not here just through the comfortable seasons, but also in the really difficult ones."

> *One of the important truths that Jesus declares is that Abba, our heavenly Father, is a vinedresser. I'm sure when He said this, the disciples' ears perked up. What's important about this is a vine-dresser was very involved in the process of the vine. Vine-dressers (also called a "husbandman") weren't merely farmers or gardeners, but were professionals in taking care of plants. The dressers' function was to nurture, prune, and provide everything needed to raise it, that it may produce lasting and healthy fruit. They were very committed to raising up good vines (vineyards) and understood that they would have to care for their vines for years. Unlike many plants we know of today, vines would live for decades. Webster calls a vinedresser as a "specialist in the area of farming." This is what Jesus was saying about His Father, that He was a*

professional when it comes to caring for the vine, His church. He loves being involved in the care, the pruning, and most of all seeing the fruit that it bears.

Aren't you glad that our vinedresser (Abba Father) doesn't treat us like an old weed, but pays attention with such detail. He's not interested in using a "crop duster" to nurture us, but He walks among us and cares for us intimately. Revelation tells us that the Son (who is the express desire of the Father), walks among the lamp stand, His church (see Revelation 1:12-13). He doesn't just pat us on the head and wish us luck, rather, He cares for each one of us with such intricate detail. He knows the number of hairs on our head and His thoughts towards us are as numerous as the sands of the sea (see Psalm 139:18). He is a good Father and vinedresser! (from 'Prayer the Great Journey')

HE DESIRES GREATER FRUIT

If you're ever in a season where it seems that He is taking things away, remember, it's because He is preparing you to bear greater fruit. He prunes the tree that bears fruit, in order to bring forth more vibrant and life-giving fruit. Those unwanted branches are removed for the sole purpose of seeing the greater ones burst forth.

One can also see the dynamics of pruning in the process of weaning, where a mother transitions her child from milk to develop its digestive system. Weaning, in all reality, is removing something from the baby's regular diet to bring the child into greater maturity and development.

No one would ever consider weaning as a negative, but a great positive. The intent of the mother is to bring a greater level of life to the child and to allow it to reach fuller potential. It would be absurd to tell the mother that her child should stay on the milk, or that the infant was being punished. On the contrary, a mother is being noble in weaning the child, for the greater purpose of maturity.

Pruning is a sign of His goodness, for He disciplines those He loves (see Hebrews 12:6). I call it "pruning unto promise," for the Lord will always deal with us according to the purpose and promises on our life. This is why discipline can vary so much from one believer to another, for He will always call us away from things that could possibly destroy us in our individual purpose.

It would be absurd for me to hand the car keys to my 15-year old son. Even if he were to ask for the car keys, I would boldly and gladly say no. Why? Because he isn't ready to get behind the wheel of a vehicle and drive around town. If I did otherwise, that would be an injustice on my part. If I chose to cave in to his immediate desire, there would be potential consequences – ones that I would definitely regret.

I remember the time in my life where I was awakened to a lifestyle of walking in signs and wonders (such as healing diseases, raising the dead, casting out devils, etc.). On the front end of this stirring, when in public, I would often look for people who were sick just so I could lay hands on them. It's fun (and scary) walking like this before Him.

When I started practicing this type of lifestyle, to be honest it was quite frustrating. I would pray for different people, and nothing would happen. Whether it was a broken foot or a common cold, many times I would walk away discouraged because that person didn't instantly receive what I had prayed for.

Several months into this, I was so discouraged and remember thinking, "This thing just isn't working." In this frustrating tension, I asked the Lord, "What's going on?" I didn't hear anything for a few days, but eventually and in His tender yet bold approach, He replied, "I haven't released some of these things yet, simply because you're not ready for it." I knew immediately what He was saying. In essence, my character wasn't developed to the point I could handle certain releases of signs and wonders through my life. In other words, if He would've allowed me to do the "greater" things I was asking for, it could've destroyed me.

Same goes with weaning – although the child may scream and throw temper tantrums, the mother knows the process will pay off in the end. To withdraw from the weaning process would be a bad decision. Even though the infant desires the milk more than life itself, the mother's follow-through will produce the intended goal of maturity. Over time, the child's craving and longings will have been altered and even more developed. The limited diet of dairy can now include other nutrients such as protein that will further strengthen the body.

God's ultimate intention for every believer is maturity. Any move that He makes in removing things from our lives, is to only enhance the process of development.

The Father longs to bring us out of the milk stage, into the fattier meats of the knowledge of God and awareness of our identity. Paul wrestled with this reality in his ministry, saying, *"And I, brethren, could not speak to you as to spiritual men, but as to men of flesh, as to infants in Christ. I gave you milk to drink, not solid food; for you were not yet able to receive it. Indeed, even now you are not yet able, for you are still fleshly. For since there is jealousy and strife among you, are you not fleshly, and are you not walking like mere men?"* 1 Corinthians 3:2 (NASB)

BEARING THE IMAGE OF ANOTHER WORLD

"So also it is written, "The first man, Adam, became a living soul." The last Adam became a life-giving spirit. However, the spiritual is not first, but the natural; then the spiritual. The first man is from the earth, earthy; the second man is from heaven. As is the earthy, so also are those who are earthy; and as is the heavenly, so also are those who are heavenly. Just as we have borne the image of the earthy, we will also bear the image of the heavenly." 1 Corinthians 15:45-49 (NASB)

Paul states that through our union with Christ, we are now the physical display of Christ in the earth.

> *"By living in God, love has been brought to its full expression in us so that we may fearlessly face the Day of Judgment, because all that Jesus now is, so are we in this world."* 1 John 4:17 (TPT)

Jesus said it this way, *"If you've seen Me, you've seen the Father* (John 14:9)." The Son of Man was stating that He was in fact, a direct reflection of the Father. When the bystanders saw Jesus healing the lame and cleansing the leper, it was all a direct act of the Father's heart to heal and cleanse. Jesus healed because His Dad did. Jesus, therefore, was an all-out display of heaven on earth. The writer of Hebrews says of Jesus, *"He is the radiance of His glory and the exact representation of His nature…"* Yes, the exact representation of the Fathers nature. Not a copy, but the original.

We are called to walk in the same spirit as Jesus did. Coming to destroy the works of the devil, He also came to show us the way to walk and live before the Father. We have always been called to represent the family business and as sons and daughters, we are to be a physical demonstration of the Father's heart to the earth.

In light of this promise, He asks us to partner with Him, that we would make the earth His place of dwelling. This is why the gifts of the Spirit are so vital, for they demonstrate and manifest the love and heart of God to the world around us. They exist to lead and connect others to a big God who is in love with His creation.

A WALKING REFLECTION

While on the earth, Jesus was a walking mirror, reflecting God's glory. Looking at Christ would be like looking at His Father. What's interesting about a mirror is its ability to reflect the frequencies of the image going into it. Blue rays go into the mirror and in turn represents blue to the natural eye, and so on. Even the movements made before it play out before our very eyes. It's quite amazing!

The science of a mirror gives us some insight…

Light is a form of energy, and when it hits a surface, such as a mirror, it is reflected or bounced from the surface. This is similar to a ball bouncing off a wall. The reflected image is comprised of photons, which are particles of light. When these photons initially hit the mirror they cause electrons to vibrate within atoms, which in turn produces an identical light photon. (from "How a Mirror Works" at ehow.com)

Jesus was an identical representation and mirror image of the Father. He perfectly presented the Father to His creation, for the same frequency going into His life came forth and presented an image of His Father. As Bill Johnson says, *"Jesus is perfect theology."* He is the exact image of the Father.

So as believers, what do we do with this reality? I'll let the scripture do the talking, for it says, *"Whoever claims to live in Him must live as Jesus did* (1 John 2:6)." You see that? As the apostle goes on to declare, the same life that He is living, we are called to live (see 1 John 4:17).

The poverty mentality says we are unqualified sinners and leaves no room to believe we can truly and fully represent the Father. However, revelation through the apostle John comes along and demolishes that lie, putting before us the possibility of walking as Jesus walked. Empowered by His Spirit, we can do the greater things that He promised.

The Greek word for "live" in 1 John 2:6 is "peripateō" meaning "go, walk about, be occupied." A root word is "pateō" meaning "to trample, crush with the feet, to advance by setting foot upon, tread upon: to encounter successfully the greatest perils from the machinations and persecutions with which Satan would fain thwart the preaching of the gospel." So, the verse would read like this: *"Whoever claims to live in Him (as a child of God) must trample and crush satan beneath their feet, just as Jesus (the beloved Son) did"* You see that now? It paints the picture of total conquest over the enemies of God, of representing and reigning.

Ephesians 2:7 tells us, *"Throughout the coming ages we will be the visible display of the infinite, limitless riches of His grace and kindness which was showered upon us in Jesus Christ."* The Greek word for "visible display" is rendered as "show" in the KJV meaning "to point out, demonstrate, prove." Because He is good, God has called us out to show forth His limitless resources and riches – He placed us on planet earth to manifest His nature. Although God could step out all by Himself on the stage and prove His sovereignty in a mere second, He still chooses weak and frail people to demonstrate it.

"Let us make man in our image" is not just a phrase found in the early days of Genesis 1. It is a perpetual and passionate cry of the Holy Spirit, as He continues to conform us into the glorious image of Jesus. He loves doing this. It is His supreme joy, and He won't stop until He has a people shining like the Son.

GOD AND FAMILY

God didn't come to establish a work force. He came because He wanted a family.

Since the beginning of time, God has always desired a family. Before He spoke light into existence, He envisioned a cosmos filled with children – sons and daughters empowered to enjoy His presence and to release His household values into the earth. This was the dream of His heart.

> *"For it was always in His perfect plan to adopt us as His delightful children, so that His tremendous grace that cascades over us would bring Him glory— for the same love He has for His Beloved One, Jesus, He has for us!"* Ephesians 1:5-6 (TPT)

Yahweh could've been consumed with simply running the cosmos as a King, but in His amazing love, desired to demonstrate His Fathering heart to the world. This is quite intriguing and makes no sense to the human mind. To take weak and broken human beings and adopt them into His household, simply confounds the wise.

Grace isn't any clearer as when He brings us into His happy, holy, and loving family. From the beginning, this was the Father's heart. We once felt the touch of the Father's hand weaving our being, and we continually long for that touch. This is why each and every person yearns for fatherly affection – we long to return to His intimate touch. It's just the way we were created.

> *"But God chose those whom the world considers foolish to shame those who think they are wise, and God chose the puny and powerless to shame the high and mighty. He chose the lowly, the laughable in the world's eyes— nobodies— so that he would shame the somebodies. For he chose what is regarded as insignificant in order to supersede what is regarded as prominent, so that there would be no place for prideful boasting in God's presence."* 1 Corinthians 1:27 (TPT)

FREE FROM CONTROL

God doesn't beat us into submission, rather He proves His devotion by wowing us with such amazing love. He never twists our arm to worship Him, instead He moves our hearts. This is the goodness of God! Never once did Jesus refer to God as a dictator or control freak, but a good Master who was first a Father. Even Jesus said of His own destiny, *"No one has taken it away from Me, but I lay it down on My own initiative. I have authority to lay it down, and I have authority to take it up again. This commandment I received from My Father* (John 10:18)."

Did you see the phrase, *"This commandment I received from My Father?"* I love how the Father instructed Jesus to willingly lay down His life on His own, free of control. In the same sense, the Father instructs us to make our own choices in life, free from control and manipulation. This is one aspect of the goodness of God. He doesn't boss us around by demanding acts of service, rather He receives freewill worship from our life by wooing us with His love and kindness.

When He wants to change our mindset, He reveals His kindness (see Romans 2:4). Just like He did with Peter in Caesarea, when He wants to transform our hearts and minds to fit inside of His realm of thinking, He speaks a Word of eternal value. When Jesus wanted to teach His disciples a lesson on *"first is last"* leadership, He broke out the bowl and began to wash their feet. He didn't retreat to a dry erase board with teaching notes and never asked anything that He wasn't willing to do Himself. Instead, He demonstrated by going low as a servant. It's just what He does.

A NEW PERSPECTIVE

"And He said, "A man had two sons. The younger of them said to his father, 'Father, give me the share of the estate that falls to me.' So he divided his wealth between them." Luke 15:1-2 (NASB)

In Luke 15, Jesus gives us three parables – the lost sheep, the lost coin, and the prodigal son. These heavenly riddles lead us to a head-on collision with the mercies of God and in all three parables, there is a hidden theme where (although displaced), none of the lost items ever lose their value. In fact, there is a party in heaven when each item is regained. The Father and His hosts are excited when one is restored to their appraised value.

One of the reasons Jesus told the parable of the prodigal son was to present a new perspective – the Father's heart to bring us into His family. The two sons represent "Christians," those who belong to the household of faith – born-again believers who went to church on Sunday and occasionally read their Bible – you know, the typical "western" Christian. However, they would represent two very different perspectives.

In telling this parable, I believe Jesus wanted to break off a slavery mentality, and bring them into a perspective of sons who belong to a loving Father. In doing so, He tells of a youngest son who leaves home to work in the fields, all to explore the "greener grass." In a sense, this son wanted to sow his wild oats, and soon realizes that this type of lifestyle is no better (and much worse) than his previous home life in the father's house. So, in his desperation, the prodigal son returns home. This part of the son coming home narrative is where the most emphasis is usually placed.

I think many of us have heard the message highlighting the fact that the son realized his brokenness and chooses to run back to the Father. It's an amazing part of the story and as of late, we've most definitely heard an overwhelming emphasis on this aspect of the Father's goodness. Although this is a very important part of the story, have you ever stopped and thought, why did the son ever leave home in the first place? What made him take such a bold step as to leave his father's house and take to the world? Pretty interesting if you ask me! Maybe he was just curious to taste the pleasures of the world, or possibly he heard that there were better options out there. Or, just maybe he had a childhood wound that went unresolved and he needed some "deliverance ministry?" Maybe a few sessions in the local prayer room or a weekend trip to Bethel would've done him some good. I know you're probably laughing right now, but these ideas I'm sure would be some of the most frequent. Let me suggest something else to you…

I personally believe the primary reason the prodigal son left home was because he had a wrong perception of the father. Instead of seeing the father as good and just, he saw him as a rigid task-master. In other words, his lens was foggy. When his perspective should've been pure, it was somehow tainted instead. Just look at the request of the prodigal son when he said, *"I want my share of your estate now before you die* (Luke 15:12)."

In those times, when a son asked the father for their inheritance, he was pretty much saying, "I wish you were dead." To cash out an inheritance before the father passed on was one of the most offensive things a son could do to a father. It wasn't just that the son was selfish, rather it revealed a deeper level of hatred and offense toward the father. Talk about dysfunction!

Interestingly, as the youngest son returns home, we see the oldest son veer off into an interesting dynamic as well. Look at his reply to what's going on: *"But he (the older son) became angry and was not willing to go in; and his father came out and began pleading with him. But he answered and said to his father, 'Look! For so many years I have been serving you and I have never neglected a command of yours; and yet you have never given me a young goat, so that I might celebrate with my friends; but when this son of yours came, who has devoured your wealth with prostitutes, you killed the fattened calf for him.'"* Luke 15:28-30 (NASB)

I believe that he, just like his younger brother, had a warped view of the father. With an offended heart, he not only counts the sin against his brother, he also refuses to enter into the house to enjoy the feast of celebration: *"he (the older son) became angry (and offended) and was not willing to go in (to what was already his)."* Furthermore, to redeem his image and reputation, the older son begins to relate to the father by his acts of obedience. In the spirit of complaining, he says, *"All these years I've slaved for you and never once refused to do a single thing you told me to. And in all that time you never gave me even one young goat for a feast with my friends. Yet when this son of yours comes back after squandering your money on prostitutes (cheap intimacy), you celebrate by killing the fattened calf!"* Luke 15:29-30 (NLT)

Do you see the offense growing as pride crosses its arms, refusing to receive the promises of the Father? One can't help but see religion creeping into the narrative. In those times, a young goat was one of the least valuable banquet delicacies, much less valuable than a lamb or a fattened calf. In essence, the older son is practically using sarcasm in response to his father. He was pretty much saying, "Gee thanks dad… you gave the runt lavish food, but have never even given me the crumbs." At this point, offense had set in as the son demands rewards (according to his self-righteous works).

With pride screaming, the oldest son starts down the road of self-promotion. Instead of allowing the father to define and affirm who he was, he enters into striving, in order to exalt his own self-importance. This, my friends, is a dangerous place. It is a slippery slope. When we go down this road of self-promotion and pride, resentment against others (and their journey) can soon follow.

Interestingly, religion will always refuse to rejoice over Gods breakthrough of grace. Out of its base of pride and self-righteousness, the spirit of religion will always demand attention for its own accolades. It'll sound something like this: "The others haven't put in the work I have. They've been doing less important things with their time. But me, I deserve better. I've slaved for you, and I should get what I've earned."

"In the culture of that era, hospitality was of supreme importance. To refuse to go in to the feast, when it was his responsibility culturally to cohost the event with his father, was a humiliating rejection of the father." (TPT commentary on Luke 15:28)

POVERTY AND PRIDE

Might I suggest, both sons needed a revelation of the father's goodness. The younger son had a view of the master through the lens of poverty, while the eldest had a view through the lens of pride. The youngest, in his frailty, perceived that he wasn't able to receive the fathers full restoration, and simply wanted to continue as a slave. The eldest refused to bask in the lavish love of his father, resisting the invitation to feast at his father's table.

Interestingly, as Jesus is pointing out, these perspectives are two thieves that stand on both sides of our position in Christ, and they wage war on what He says over us. The prevailing voice of Christ saying, *"It is finished,"* is always met by the poverty and prideful mentality. The youngest son thought he had to do more to obtain considerable favor from the father while the older thought he had already done enough. One son was bound as a slave while the other was locked up with self.

THE FATHER'S RELENTLESS PURSUIT

Still yet, the father did not cease to pursue his sons. It's interesting how, in the midst of a warped view, the Father's mercy will chase us down and reveal both the prideful and poverty mindset. It doesn't tolerate either one, but pursues us until we are a surrendered soul. As Jesus is articulating, His grace is so tenacious and furious in uncovering what stands in its way. Although we may try to hide behind the veil of fear and shame, we will never be able to escape the goodness and mercy of God. It follows us all the days of our lives (see Psalm 23:6).

As this parable further reveals, although the Father continues to take hits against His nature, He still pursues His children. Both sons rejected the father's goodness, as his invitation to simply be a celebrated son was met with the hardened heart of fear and shame, pride and poverty. However, we serve a God who is secure in Himself – the Father isn't threatened by our weak and vulnerable hearts. Even though He continues to be betrayed, He isn't pacing the halls of heaven wondering who He is. Instead, He continues to extend His heart and hand to us. In our broken and frail state, He still continues to invite us into the feast. It's just what He does!

Religion refuses to go to feasts, while relationship plunges right into it.

There is nothing wrong with seeing God as a good Master as long as we see Him through the eyes of sonship. Viewing God as a good Master is fine, but seeing Him as a good Father is foundational. Even Paul referred to believers as "servants." However, he did so through the lens of first being the beloved. This is why he calls us "bondservants." In Biblical times, bondservants were different than slaves; (hence the word "bond" implying covenant and promise). At the end of the servants' appointed time of service, they had to make a decision to go or stay with the master. In most cases, if the servant enjoyed them and desired to stay, they would willfully remain on staff. The bondservant was basically putting their life in the hands of the master, indicating that the servant had a healthy view and even a good relationship with his master. From this point, the servant would enter into a bond (covenant) with the master.

> *"If the servant declares, 'I love my master and my wife and children and do not want to go free,' then his master must take him before the judges. He shall take him to the door or the doorpost and pierce his ear with an awl. Then he will be his servant for life."* Exodus 21:5-6 (ESV)

FREEWILL SERVICE

Bondservants went on to give their time and labor out of desire, not demand. Once a bondservant, they were viewed as one of the (covenant) family members, and thus became recipients of the inheritor's promise. Instead of working for the master, the bondservant understood that he worked with him. While slaves work for favor, bondservants work from it. One works as a pauper, the other as a partner. They labor from the place of knowing the master's desire, not just His commands. Therefore, when we walk in close fellowship with the Father (as bondservants), we respond to His desire.

I have such an amazing dad – along with being my biological father, he is a spiritual one and also my best friend. We walk together on so many levels and I know any time I need encouragement, he is always there to give it. I trust him and I know that he is out to see the best for me. In our relationship, there are times that I want to do something for him that is out of the ordinary. I find no duty in doing the extraordinary things for him. In fact, it is a joy to do so. Why? Simply because he and I have a relationship established in love and friendship. I am out to see the best for him and I know he feels the same.

The calling to be a disciple is always a call to be part of His family. When

Jesus invited the disciples into following Him, He was actually inviting them to be sons – a love affair with our Father in heaven. In a sense, they were His 12 bondservants. This is especially clear at the last supper (see Matthew 26:26-29).

Bill Johnson says, *"The disciples belonged before they believed."* We can't separate this reality from the Gospel, or relegate this type of ministry to a certain local body. We are all called to cultivate a family dynamic in our lives. When one looks at the book of Acts, you can't help but see family and oneness at the heart of what God was doing through the hands of the church.

"And all those who had believed were together and had all things in common; and they began selling their property and possessions and were sharing them with all, as anyone might have need. Day by day continuing with one mind in the temple, and breaking bread from house to house, they were taking their meals together with gladness and sincerity of heart." Acts 2:44-46 (**NASB**)

A great miracle of the Holy Spirit in Acts wasn't just that He raised the dead or that He opened up cities for the Gospel – it was that He united a diverse people, setting them in one mind and one accord. The miracle of getting (zealous and ambitious) human beings on the same page is something that is only possible by the wisdom of heaven. (from 'Acts : A Unified Church')

OUR FATHER IN HEAVEN

I love the prayer that Jesus taught us in Matthew 6! Many call it the "Lord's Prayer," but Jesus instructed us to pray for the release of sins, and He never sinned, so I think it needs to be called the "family prayer." Interestingly, before Jesus taught us what to pray, He first taught us to lift our gaze to the One to whom we are praying. In other words, it was more important to understand *Who* we are praying to, than *what* we are praying.

When Jesus said, *"Our Father,"* He was declaring, "Turn your eyes to the head of the family, the One who has caused redeemed sons and daughters to come before Him."

Jesus is a good Son because He has a good Father. As the Father's delight, Jesus knew He had the attention of His Father. This is why He addressed Him with a heart of thanksgiving. When Jesus prayed, He locked eyes with the One in whom His soul delighted. Never do we see Jesus reacting in fear to please the Father, nor do we see Him whimpering around with His eyes downward. Rather, He lifted His eyes in wholehearted attention to Abba. He prayed looking up (see John 11:41 & 17:1).

I think sometimes we approach the Father with our lists, and we miss out on the reality of enjoying His heart of delight over us. We often come asking and asking, when we just need to come beholding. Both are equally important, but are incomplete when they are separate. During my concentrated times of prayer and devotion, I often like to start my time just beholding Him. I'll usually take 15-20 minutes just meditating on who He is. Many times it's without words, and just a simple gaze on His goodness. Instead of barging in and asking for my list of things, I will boldly come to simply look on the One who my soul loves. Over the years, I've found it to be my favorite dynamic in prayer.

As we move forward, this is one thing we must settle in our hearts. Not just in this book, but in our walk with the Lord. It is imperative that we see ourselves in Christ and sharing in the same inheritance that Jesus did. We are sons who share in the delight of the Father. Let the sons and daughters rejoice!

Pray this with me: *Abba, I receive You as the good and loving Father. Right now, I let down any walls that would keep me from seeing you any other way. Wash my heart and my mind in this revelation. In Jesus' name!*

9

CHILDREN OF INHERITANCE

"Do not be afraid, little flock, for your Father has chosen gladly to give you the kingdom." Luke 12:32 (NASB)

As we have been discussing, much of our identity hinges on inheritance – that which has been given to us in Christ, and what has been given to Christ that now resides in us. It's one thing to understand that we have things in Christ that we are seeking after, yet it's another thing to know we have things in us that Christ is seeking after. He is the glory of our inheritance and, at the same time, we are the glory of His inheritance. In other words, He has treasure in us and we have treasure in Him.

Therefore, our pursuit is like a perpetual "round and round we go." This type of pursuit is the heart of Song of Songs, (see chapters 4 & 5) and is why Paul prayed for the church of Ephesus to enter into the realm of revelation. He knew once their eyes were opened to their inheritance in Christ, many issues related to life would fall into place.

"...that the God of our Lord Jesus Christ, the Father of glory, may give to you a spirit of wisdom and of revelation in the knowledge of Him. I pray that the eyes of your heart may be enlightened, so that you will know what is the hope of His calling,

what are the riches of the glory of His inheritance in the saints, and what is the surpassing greatness of His power toward us who believe." Ephesians 1:17-18 (NASB)

In Psalm 2, we have the privilege of experiencing dialogue between God the Father, God the Son, and God the Holy Spirit. All three Persons speak throughout its verses, in an orchestrated expression of their desire. In this passage, under divine inspiration of the Holy Spirit, David declares Abba's supreme desire of glorifying His Son among the nations. Out of Their intimate fellowship, the Father summons the Son to ask for His inheritance in the nations: *"Ask of Me, and I will surely give the nations as Your inheritance, and the very ends of the earth as Your possession."* The Father longs to hear the Son speak of His desires and beckons Him to ask. I can see the Father leaning over to His Son's throne and saying, "My Son, what would you like… what's your desire? Just tell me Son, and I'll do it!" Can you imagine what that prayer meeting was like?

I dream of a day when more of that type of intimate fellowship fills our prayer meetings – where we lock eyes with our heavenly Father and ask for the things that are directly on His heart. Prayer meetings that mirror the Trinity's love for one another and for mankind! Worship gatherings where the desire of the nations (for Jesus to come) is a direct correlation of Jesus' desire to captivate the nations. Lord, fill our prayer meetings with the desire that You and the Father share.

JACOB AND ESAU

In the history of Israel, we have two characters of grave importance – Jacob and Esau. In the unfolding narrative, Jacob became Israel and Esau became Edom. Israel represents promise while Edom represents that which wars against the promise. Remember, it was Esau who sold his birthright for a bowl of soup, compromising the promise that he was to receive. This act escalated into open resentment and hostility – one man's compromise soon became an entire tribe's resistance of the people of God. Eventually, Edom was constantly warring against Gods destiny and His Word over Israel. While the Lord was calling His people into the promised land, Edom was striving to keep them out. Interestingly, Scripture tells us that the two brothers (of opposition) in Rebekah's womb were actually two nations.

> *"The Lord said to her, 'Two nations are in your womb; and two peoples will be separated from your body; and one people shall be stronger than the other; and the older shall serve the younger.'"* Genesis 25:23 (**NASB**)

As scripture tells us, Jacob desired the inheritance so much that he set up a whole deceiving act for his father. Not only did he stir up confusion in Esau, he also released an avalanche of controversy and strife. In essence, this was a bad family split.

Today, the Edomite spirit is jealous of our inheritance and longs to keep us ignorant and unaware of it. This religious spirit doesn't mind us talking about it or even being curious about our portion in Christ, as long as we don't touch or manifest it in our walk. It will allow us to host conferences and workshops on identity, as long as we don't take the ground therein. The enemy knows that once the children of God understand their place in the family of God, his plan is revealed and ultimately vanquished.

TWO OPPOSING VIEWS

Just as Rebekah had two opposing siblings in her womb (see Genesis 25:23), so we always have two paradigms (of the Spirit and flesh) at war within us. Paul says, *"The sinful nature wants to do evil, which is just the opposite of what the Spirit wants. And the Spirit gives us desires that are the opposite of what the sinful nature desires. These two forces are constantly fighting each other, so you are not free to carry out your good intentions."* Galatians 5:17 (**NLT**)

The Spirit-led life is where God contends and we rest, while the flesh-dominated life is where man contends and God resists. The Lord said to Rebekah, *"One people shall be stronger than the other; and the older shall serve the younger."* Remember, the stronger one was Jacob, while the weaker was Esau. In other words, God is saying, "I made you stronger and victorious. Now from that reality, wrestle against wrong mindsets, not against me. I've called you to war against principalities and strongholds, only to manifest my victory and strength through you."

THE OPTION TO RULE

Many of us know the story of Cain and Abel. It's another account of two contrary views, as Cain offered up an unpleasing sacrifice while his brother offered up an acceptable one. In the swirl of Cain's raging fit, the Lord stepped in to calm him down, saying, *"If you do well, will not your countenance be lifted up? And if you do not do well, sin is crouching at the door; and its desire is for you, but you must master (rule, have dominion over) it* (Genesis 4:7)." Like a toddler who's just lost his favorite toy, Cain was out of control and in a moment of decision, the Lord commands him with the option of mastering the moment. He urges Cain to take that passion and instead of raging, the Lord attempts to direct it toward ruling. I wish I could say that Cain took the Lord's counsel, but we know he didn't.

Paul told the church, *"In your anger, do not sin."* Apparently, Paul was trying to encourage them to channel anger the right way. This tells me it's not a sin to become angry, it's only normal. However, the judgment is passed on how we respond when anger arises. The emotion of anger isn't bad, only the negative application of it. I look at human emotions as a river. Just as we have a river living inside of us, how we direct those raging waters, determines the results. We can fill the well with righteousness or we can pollute it with lesser things. The decision is ours to make.

WORSHIP AND DOMINION

The cosmos spins with eager anticipation for sons and daughters to awaken and take their place. Creation knows that once the children of God arise, the earth finds it's eternal purpose as a resting place for the Lord. Why you might ask? Why would creation, the work of God's hands, look to frail men and women to arise into their place as His children? It comes down to the fact that man was called to bring the earth under subjection to the Lord. This was the Lord's mandate from day one. David says in Psalm 115:16, *"He has given us the earth and put us in charge."* As the Lord created it, we were called to help conduct it.

In Romans 1, Paul lays out the story of mankind's rebellion and the forfeited mandate of ruling:

"For since the creation of the world His invisible attributes, His eternal power and divine nature, have been clearly seen, being understood through what has been made, so that they are without excuse. For even though they knew God, they did not honor Him as God or give thanks, but they became futile in their speculations, and their foolish heart was darkened. Professing to be wise, they became fools, and exchanged the glory of the incorruptible God for an image in the form of corruptible man and of birds and four-footed animals and crawling creatures. Therefore God gave them over in the lusts of their hearts to impurity, so that their bodies would be dishonored among them. For they exchanged the truth of God for a lie, and worshiped and served the creature rather than the Creator, who is blessed forever. Amen." Romans 1:20-25 (**NASB**)

In his opening statement to the Roman believers, Paul is stating that men fell into worship of one another (and animals) – they worshipped the image rather than the source. Instead of being entertained by the glory of the Lord, they became fascinated with the glory of creation. The wonder reserved for Yahweh, became misguided in worship of His design.

"Idol" is another word for "image" in the Bible, and speaks of a figure that point us to a greater power. In some parts of the world, they believe idols are images that release the virtues of the greater power. In other words, they look to the idol to extend healing and the goodness of that represented power. Idols aren't inherently bad, it's the aim and affection toward the idol that can be in error. In fact, we are "God's idols," images created to show forth His power and majesty – leading others to pursue the "greater power" (see 1 Peter 2:9 & Psalm 50:2).

When the Lord commissioned man from the garden, He told him to rule and subdue what He had created. The divine order that He set in motion in the beginning is God to man, and man to creation. Man is called to live in intimacy with God first and foremost, extending that love into the earth. In other words, man is called to be a heavenly conduit, a divinely orchestrated symphony of Christ's peace. We are to hear the song of the Lamb and bring that symphony into the earth. This demands that we come into alignment with the sound of His heart, which is learned in the place of intimacy, worship, and adoration.

Furthermore, worship manifests our authority in Christ. It keeps our hearts aligned with the Commander in Chief. As we align through worship with our Creator, we can rightly rule and extend His rule into the earth. In other words, it's all about INTIMACY and AUTHORITY.

As we worship regularly, we will rule rightly.

The earth (creation) wants to submit to mankind, for it is the creative design of the Father. It was made with the innate desire to be ruled over and hasn't rebelled or refused to receive sons and daughters as its leader. Instead, it groans and waits in the eager expectation of burning intensity for us to take our place and be revealed as His children (see Romans 8:19). In other words, it cries out for the divine order to be restored, where man is in fellowship with God, and rules the earth from that place of intimate communion.

I know we have preachers who gladly proclaim the burning fires of hell. What if we had preachers who, with greater intensity, declared to the church, the burning intensity of creation for the children of God to take their place. What if we had teachers and divine instructors who awoken the church to heavens' eager expectation for sons and daughters to arise. Religion trembles at the revelation of sonship. When the (worshipping and adoring) children of God awaken to their identity in the beloved Son, anything contrary to that has to bow its weak knee.

Jesus declared that if we refuse to lift our voices, creation would cry out (see Luke 19:40). In other words, if we as sons and daughters don't worship, creation has to step out of its divine order to ensure God gets what is due Him. Creation was designed to inspire worship, and never to receive it. The beautiful creation we see should cause our hearts and eyes to aim upward.

THE ORPHAN SPIRIT

Once sons and daughters arise, all things are possible. The enemy knew this early on, so he labored to create an orphan mentality in the hearts of men. Being an orphan himself, he worked from a jealous and polluted position. Forfeiting his design of joining creation in worship, he began his rampage of creating distortion and chaos in the workmanship of God.

Orphan can be defined as "a child whose parents are dead." The absence of a family is the central idea. As a result, orphans lack inheritance, rights, and sometimes a home. This, in a spiritual sense, is the tragedy of not knowing Jesus – wandering aimlessly with no purpose, inheritance, or rights of belonging to a family. On the contrary, sons and daughters carry the name and nature of the Father. Furthermore, when you get His name, you also get His resources (wisdom, power, riches, etc.).

Because my name is Atwood, I belong to a family and I am now in line to receive all that belongs to my father. In other words, the name I bear releases the resources that my father has. This, I believe, is why Solomon cried out for God's name to be on the temple (house of prayer), for as it bore the name of God, it would also represent the nature, resources, and heart of God.

The enemy, in his craftiness, promptly began creating wrong mindsets in mankind. We see this clearly in Genesis 4, where he begins by stirring jealousy and strife in the bloodline between Cain and Abel. Once Cain gave into the temptation, God declared the consequences of his actions. Out of the response of shame, Cain began adding consequences that God didn't declare. In a sense, the enemy (through Cain) began adding words to the mouth of Yahweh. Let's look at the text…

> *"The Lord said, "What have you done? Listen! Your brother's blood cries out to me from the ground. Now you are under a curse and driven from the ground, which opened its mouth to receive your brother's blood from your hand. When you work the ground, it will no longer yield its crops for you. You will be a restless wanderer on the earth." Cain said to the Lord, "My punishment is more than I can bear. Today you are driving me from the land, and <u>I will be hidden from your presence</u>; I will be a restless wanderer on the earth, and <u>whoever finds me will kill me</u>. But the Lord said to him, "Not so; anyone who kills Cain will suffer vengeance seven times over." Then the Lord put a mark on Cain so that no one who found him would kill him. So Cain went out from the Lord's presence and lived in the land of Nod, east of Eden."* Genesis 4:10-16 (**NIV**)

Did you notice how Cain added consequences to his disobedience. (see the above underlined part). He replies to the Lord saying, *"I will be hidden from Your presence."* Yahweh didn't say that! While the Lord declared the consequence of being a wanderer and unfruitful farmer, He never took His presence away from Cain. The Lord quickly replies, *"Not so"* and then releases a promise of protection over him. Although the Lord was allowing the consequence of sin to take its course, in no way was He driving Cain from His presence. Instead, I believe Yahweh desired to bring redemption to his life. He didn't want to banish Cain, He desired to bring him closer. Isn't that what the Father always desires to do?

Adding conditions to the spoken word of God is one of the primary signs of an orphan spirit. It can't receive the free gift of grace, and tries to add stipulations in order to bind up our freedom. Through this lens, we can see that Cain was a type of the orphan spirit. He was the firstborn, yet failed to realize it. He related to God through a skewed lens. Just as Cain worked the flesh (the ground, a cursed element), so the orphan spirit feeds on the flesh – competition, fear, self-promotion. If it can get you in competition or fear mode, it will wrestle you into a place of submission. The enemy's ultimate aim is to convince you that the Father has banished you from His presence. Although the Father will allow consequences and discipline to take its course, He will never banish His children from His presence.

JOSPEH'S BROTHERS: A TYPE OF THE ORPHAN SPIRIT

Joseph's brothers refused to receive him, and instead sought to kill him. Instead of getting behind his God-given dream, they mocked and ultimately sought to destroy him. They stripped Joseph's robe (Genesis 37:23), and removed his water source (37:24). This represents a type of the orphan spirit. Just like the brothers of Joseph, the orphan spirit longs to steal, kill, and destroy your destiny. Fueled by jealousy and strife, it stands in direct opposition to confident sons and daughters. Through ridicule and accusation, it labors to wear down the children of God. You can always recognize the orphan spirit when you encounter some of the following traits.

Signs of an orphan spirit:

- Competition (Comparison)
- Self-promotion
- Jealousy
- Fear
- Insecurity

Do you see any of these traits in your life? If so, pause and ask Holy Spirit to open your eyes to the schemes of the enemy and to reveal the glorious plans of the Father. Cast your care upon Him, for He wants to take them and open your eyes to what He says is available. He hasn't given you anything but that which touches the realm of power, love, and a sound mind.

"For God has not given us a spirit of fear, but of power and of love and of a sound mind." 2 Timothy 1:7 (NKJV)

There is a plot in the counsel of darkness, to overthrow and bind up sons and daughters. However, there is a Son who has broken the power of darkness, to restore sons and daughters back into the family. He came to give us His name and nature.

Abel brought sacrifice, while Cain brought convenience. Orphans will always bring something that is easy and from the leftover pile. To the orphan spirit, there is no surplus, only a lack of resources and riches. Instead of basking in the overflow of the Father's goodness and resources, the orphan spirit labors to gather everything for itself – stockpiling self-promotion and personal fame. This leaves no room for legacy and generational blessing.

IF YOU'RE THE SON OF GOD

Many times, satan attempts to create confusion and chaos by questioning our identity as sons and daughters. This is especially true when we're in the wilderness of life. In doing so, he will often attach it with works – getting us striving and in performance mode. If the enemy gets us thinking "do" instead of "be," he can distort our reason for existence – it's an ancient accusation (see Genesis 3). In the 40-day wilderness testing, interestingly satan tried to get Jesus to perform. When tempting Jesus with turning stones into bread and hurling Himself from the temple, twice he said to Jesus, *"If You are the Son of God..."*

It's interesting, however, that satan didn't use *"If You are the Son of God"* when tempting Jesus with worship. Instead, he leaves that part out. What was happening here? Why would the accuser use *"If You are the Son of God"* in two temptations while not using it in the worship one? Could it be that there was something specific happening here?

I personally believe that when the devil tempted Jesus with worship, he was aiming at the humanity of Christ. While the other two temptations dealt with Jesus' divinity (as the Son of God), the worship temptation was dealing with Christ's humanity (as the Son of man). This reveals the free will of worship, for when we worship, we are taking our (freewill) humanity and aiming it at the divinity of God. In other words, worship is the act of bringing heaven and earth together. This is why worship is so powerful.

Think about it... satan was given the keys because of Adam and Eve's mishandling of the enemy's lies. Therefore, in His humanity and divinity, the greater Adam came to repossess it. Led and empowered by the Spirit, Jesus destroyed the works of the devil in the wilderness, manifesting it in His death and resurrection (see 1 John 3:8). And He did it from the basis of worship unto the Father.

Matthew 4 calls satan the accuser, meaning he is the one who files charges against God's people. Day and night, he accuses us with wrongdoing, for his continual language is lies. It is his native tongue and he knows no other way to talk (see John 8:44). There's a joke in the South that says, "You know a liar is lying when his mouth is moving." This implies that you never trust a liar. Same goes with the accuser of the brethren – anything coming from his mouth is a lie. Period! His words carry no merit whatsoever, and we need not listen to or trust his voice in any way.

HEARING THE FATHER

Many believers who walk in fear often question if they hear God. They spend countless hours and days contemplating if God cares or even listens to them. This, I believe, is one of the leading causes of fear and worry. Friends, if you can perceive a spirit of fear, then you can hear the Father. You just have to tune into the right frequency. The question isn't, "Do I hear God," but "What frequency am I on?" Many times we can test the frequency of our station by taking inventory of the incoming signals. Maybe they're human opinions, distorted teaching, or even just too many mediocre things that cloud our thinking. Whatever the case, it is good for us to do frequent inventory of the signal that we are allowing into our ear-gate.

Prayer: *Holy Spirit, what signals am I allowing into my life? Search my heart and make room for the Father's voice. In Jesus' name.*

JESUS AND SONSHIP

Jesus was tuned into the frequency of His Father's voice. He heard the rhythm and felt the movements of His heart. This is why He says, *"I do nothing but what I see the Father doing, I say nothing but what I see the Father doing* (John 5:19)." In other words, Jesus was a real-time image of our Father in heaven. If one saw Jesus doing or saying something, it was because His Father was doing or saying it. This is why Jesus did various miracles in each place – for what was fitting and on God's heart for one place, would be different than what's on His heart for the next.

Nevertheless, all that Christ did (healing the sick, raising the dead, etc.) was from the place of Sonship. Therefore, His identity wasn't in what He did, but who He was. Jesus knew whose He was and who He was. He had no inward conflict because He knew He was the object of the Father's delight. The voice of affirmation is what preceded His ministry action. Before Christ was led, He was first affirmed, and when this took place, the rest was history!

"And a voice from heaven said, "This is my Son, whom I love; with him I am well pleased." Matthew 3:17 (NIV)

"Then Jesus was led by the Spirit into the wilderness to be tempted by the devil." Matthew 4:1 (NIV)

It is interesting that Peter's revelation of Jesus was one of Sonship; he answered Christ saying, *"You are Christ, the SON of the living God."* Of all the names that the young disciple could've called Jesus, he says *"You are… the Son…"* He could've said, "Jesus, You are the Prince of Peace; the Holy One of Israel," or he could've emphatically replied, "You are the Lord of hosts." Since Jesus is all things perfect, he could've thrown any powerful name out there and it would've been correct. However, it wouldn't have been right for the moment. Jesus was looking for a certain reply that only the Father in heaven could unveil, and in a moment, Abba peeled back the curtain and revealed His Son. He rent the veil of revelation and introduced His beloved Son to the onlooking disciples.

Jesus makes it clear that the revelation of Sonship would be the very bedrock on which He would build His church. It would be a rock that no storm could prevail against, a reality that would continue to set the people of God apart.

> *"Jesus replied, 'you are favored and privileged Simeon, son of Jonah! For you didn't discover this on your own, but My Father in heaven has supernaturally revealed it to you. I give you the name Peter the Rock. And this truth of who I am will be the bedrock foundation on which I will build My church – My legislative assembly, and the power of death will not be able to overpower it. I will give you the keys of heaven's Kingdom realm to forbid on earth that which is forbidden in heaven, and to release that which is released in heaven."* Matthew 16:17-19 (TPT)

INVITED INTO THE FELLOWSHIP

In the Matthew 6 prayer, Jesus turned the disciples' attention to the Father in heaven, for He knew if they developed a prayer life with Abba, it would lead to a deeper revelation and unveiling of who He was. Remember, Jesus said, *"Flesh and blood did not reveal this to you, but MY FATHER who is in heaven* (Matthew 16:17b)." In other words, once we discover the Father, we discover the Son. Simply said, They lead us to one another. In no way are They threatened by each other's leadership style, but are eager to glorify and reveal the other to mankind.

By teaching them to pray, *"Our Father in heaven,"* He was inviting them into the eternal fellowship of Father and Son. I can hear Him saying, "Come on in fellas, enter into Our fellowship…it'll revolutionize your life." For hundreds of years, mankind had developed a slave-to-master relationship with God. Therefore, Jesus came to shatter that view and bring us into the fullness of love and fellowship (see 1 John 1:3-4). Jesus' life on earth was an open display of Father-Son fellowship and for three decades, mankind was taken behind the veil, to see Father and Son connect. Jesus did this not only as a natural overflow of love, but also to show us the better way.

He loves the Son so much that He has handed all authority over to Him.

"All things have been handed over to Me by My Father; and no one knows the Son except the Father; nor does anyone know the Father except the Son, and anyone to whom the Son wills to reveal Him." Matthew 11:27 (NASB)

Since the Father loves the Son with an unimaginable love, He saw it fit to bring us front-row:

"For the Father loves the Son, and shows Him all things that He Himself is doing; and the Father will show Him greater works than these, so that you will marvel." John 5:20 (NASB)

WHO DO YOU SAY THAT I AM

10

SONS AND DAUGHTERS ARISING

"For the creation waits with eager longing for the revealing of the sons of God."
Romans 8:19 (ESV)

I have to admit, I am one proud father! Misty and I have always been our children's biggest cheerleaders. Whether they're playing sports or music, you can clearly see it come out. Just recently, they both played their first prayer room set for a large audience at the house of prayer. While they played and sang, I caught myself standing in the media booth throwing my hands up – not only in praise to the Lord, but also in cheering them on.

My children bring me so much joy, and although it is a little difficult watching them grow up, it is also pleasing to see them step into greater maturity and potential. My heart as a father is to steward and develop their calling to love God, love people, and walk in their divine calling.

Although I'm cheering on my own children's development and maturity, there's a much louder reality of cheering going on from creation – for the sons and daughters of God to arise. Romans tells us that creation is cheering on our formation as the manifest sons and daughters of God. The Spirit cries within us, while creation groans around us, looking for those who walk in their identity as sons – longing to display the fellowship that Jesus and Abba shared (see Romans 8:19).

Jesus is the model. He is the image of what is available inside of a life with God, as we are empowered by the Spirit of God. He shows us the impossibilities being possible. In light of this, each believer should be a glimpse into what God has available for the earth. The resources that dwell in Christ dwell in us. In other words, He wants the Kingdom that dwells within us to be the Kingdom that manifests around us.

"Each Christian's physical presence on this planet is a literal portal into eternity, a glimpse into the "other side," a connection for the people around them to the blessings, love, and gifts that God wants to spread throughout the earth... No matter how we describe it, each of us individually represents, very literally, concentrations of God's character and life force in space-time toward the people we encounter." (From "Prayer, Quantum Physics and Hotel Mattresses" by Jim Berge)

CIRCUMSTANCES AND "LIFE"

If anyone had the right to opt out in the time of great testing, Jesus did. Think about it. One of His first sermons had Him thrown out of the city, with attempted murder by the religious leaders (see Luke 4:29). Yeah, the leading scholars of the day wanted to ring His neck, literally! Still yet, God's Son remained focused on the task at hand, by being about the Father's business. He didn't allow His circumstances to dictate His stance – instead, He allowed His place in God to keep Him focused and faithful. It's also interesting that Paul, in his letters, spent minimal time bringing attention to his adverse circumstances and instead, he spent a majority of his writing focusing on our stance in Christ.

"Circumstance" is a compound word, formed from "circum" and "stance". Circum means, "surrounding or encircling," while stance means, "a person's posture." When you combine these words, you get the idea that circumstances are "situations surrounding a person's posture." In other words, they are the winds (of advantage or adversity) that swirl around us while we are standing. Let that sink in for a moment. How many times do we allow storms or successes brewing around us to affect our stance?

I marvel at the fact that although Jesus was severely tested, he was never shaken. He stayed the course of sonship, never wavering on the eternal truth that He was His Father's favorite. Rather, it seemed as if the storms brewing around Him actually set a firmer resolve in Him to complete His Father's mission. Again, His greatest testing (aside from the cross) was the wilderness temptations, and may I remind you that, after intense resistance, the Son of God came out swinging. He didn't wobble out of the desert navel gazing in a pity party, rather Luke tells us this: *"And Jesus returned to Galilee in the power of the Spirit, and news about Him spread through all the surrounding district."* Luke 4:14 (NASB)

Christ came out of testing with a brighter and more intense devotion to the mission He was sent to accomplish.

With Jesus as our great example, we can't allow external pressure and circumstances to dictate our stance in the Lord, nor can we allow them to shape our thoughts about who He is. I've often seen the church form certain theologies by what God did or didn't do in a certain setting. For example, if someone didn't get healed like we expected or a breakthrough didn't come in the timing hoped, we can often form errors of thought to support that disappointment. It can happen to any of us.

TESTING MY PERSPECTIVE

It was in the fall of 2008, that I underwent one of the greatest times of testing in my life. Misty and I had just bought a new house, and months before, I had also started a new job that included a significant increase in pay. This was all on top of our little baby girl, Olivia, being born earlier that year. It was an exciting time in our life. I mean, more money, new job, new baby – we felt like we were on top of the world. It was looking good until one day, my new job took a turn for the worse. Through a series of events, one of the "high up" employees practically turned against me and had my position eliminated. With a significant pay increase, we had practically built our life around my new job. What I thought was a major promotion and time of favor, ended up being an outpouring of pruning in my life.

So, in my ambition to overcome and get our house in order (to offset the job loss), I set out to lower our expenses. First thing on the list was to buy Misty a cheaper vehicle. I figured it was a start to cutting our bills. So, within a few days I had found an SUV at an auction in West Virginia – at the time I was traveling there, wholesaling vehicles for a living. On my way home from the auction with her new (but cheaper) 2003 Ford Explorer, I heard a loud noise in the rear of the vehicle. I looked in my rear view to find smoke billowing up. Thinking the car was on fire, I immediately pulled over. Fortunately, the car wasn't on fire, just broken down. As I sat on the exit ramp of I-75, I remember just laying my head on the steering wheel, wondering if any of this storm was going to cease. These situations individually carried little effect, but when you put them all together in the world of job-loss, it seemed like everything was crashing in.

All of the sudden, the season of joy shifted to a time of brokenness and depression. I had never dealt with depression up to this point, and other than crying, I had no grid for dealing with it. Before I knew it, my vision became very cloudy. Within days, I found myself in a deep dark funk, unable to shake the feeling of hopelessness. I felt like the weight of the world was on my shoulders and the trust I believed to have, was being tested.

Although there are those who go through much more intense pressure and shaking, the point is, circumstances can often shake our view of who God is and who we are to Him. The "circums" of life can often dictate our "stance." It's just part of being human. However, I never want seasons of disappointment to change my view of God. I never want my vision to be skewed from the reality that He is good and always in favor of breakthrough and transformation. Instead, I want to stay constant in the "stance" that He is my advantage in the midst of adversity. He is all things good and always wants to see His children prosper in mind, soul and body (see 3 John 1:2). In other words, He is our biggest cheerleader!

IN THE BOOKS: OUR LEGAL STANDING IN CHRIST

In his writings to the Romans, Paul used a lot of legal terminology to get his point across. Relating to the ministries of grace and law, Romans could be viewed as the most legal-saturated book of the Bible. In hopes to relay the Gospel message to the lofty and intellectual thinkers of Rome, Paul gets on their level. This is why we see words like "justification, condemnation, law, reconciliation" – legal terms used in the court systems today (see Romans 3:20, 28; 8:3-4).

In his opening statement, Paul begins by building a case of guilt concerning men and womens' rebellion. In other words, Paul wanted to contrast an unredeemed life in rebellion, versus a redeemed one in Christ. To build the narrative, he craftily paints the picture of guilt and reveals the heaped-up pile of shame that weighed on mankind's shoulders. In the first chapter alone, he quickly proves the need for redemption and reconciliation.

"For the wrath of God is revealed from heaven against all ungodliness and unrighteousness of men, who suppress the truth in unrighteousness, because what may be known of God is manifest in them, for God has shown it to them. For since the creation of the world His invisible attributes are clearly seen, being understood by the

things that are made, even His eternal power and Godhead, so that they are without excuse, because, although they knew God, they did not glorify Him as God, nor were thankful, but became futile in their thoughts, and their foolish hearts were darkened. Professing to be wise, they became fools, and changed the glory of the incorruptible God into an image made like corruptible man – and birds and four-footed animals and creeping things." Romans 1:18-23 (NKJV)

When someone is convicted (found guilty), the court system takes legal action. The plaintiff and defendant gather to start the process of making a plea. In the end, the most substantial evidence wins. This is how it went with us, as the Father stepped in to take legal action. With tattered garments and dirty robes, the weight of shame was just too much for man to approach the Father's throne. We were guilty. But as we see in Revelation 5, Jesus the only One found worthy, approached on our behalf. As heaven's perfect representative, this Man took on the most complex case and went to work. Now, through His death and resurrection, we have been made righteous and free. As we put our faith in the One who made our plea, we are now justified to a seated position. Praise God, we have a heavenly and humanly representative who has fought and won on our behalf!

"And through the divine authority of His cross, He cancelled out every legal violation we had on our record and the old arrest warrant that stood to indict us. He erased it all – our sins, our stained soul, and our shameful failure to keep His laws – He deleted it all and they cannot be retrieved! Everything we once were in Adam has been placed onto His cross and nailed permanently there as a public display of cancellation!" Colossians 2:14 (TPT)

HIS VICTORY ON DISPLAY

In ancient times when Paul was writing this letter, conquering kings would make the announcement of victory by conducting a public spectacle of their conquered enemy. It was an all-out party celebrating the conquering kings' might and strength. Amidst the celebration of people in their city and sphere of leadership, the procession would be followed by the noblemen of their day. In Colossians 2, Paul ties our freedom to this act of public procession:

> *"Then Jesus made a public spectacle of all the powers and principalities of darkness, stripping away from them every weapon and all their spiritual authority and power to accuse us. And by the power of the cross, Jesus led them around as prisoners in a procession of triumph! He was not their prisoner; they were His!"* Colossians 2:15 (TPT)

Even further back in history, when a king overthrew an opposing kingdom, he would sever a piece of the king's robe and attach it to his own. This would signify that the victorious king had stripped the opposing king of his authority. The longer robe a king had usually signified his exponential victories and supreme authority over other kingdoms. This is why Isaiah said, *"In the year of King Uzziah's death I saw the Lord sitting on a throne, lofty and exalted, with the train of His robe filling the temple* (Isaiah 6:1 NASB)." His kingly robe filled the temple!

According to historians, the temple in Isaiah's day was approximately 20 stories, reaching over 200 feet in height. In other words, Isaiah was having a vision of the victorious King, who had overcome all opposing kings and kingdoms. Being so vast, His robe filled a 20 story worship center. Now, that's a big God!

King Uzziah (who indulged in pagan practice) represented anything that hinders our walk with God. In other words, I hear Isaiah saying something like this: "I saw hinderances of the knowledge of God annihilated, and I saw the Lord lifted high. I saw the glory of the Lord (His resurrection, victory, and power) on display." We could say it this way, "In the year that religion died, I saw the Lord lifted high..." or "In the year that fear died, I saw the Lord lifted high." This is why I believe Isaiah 6 is not just a good story of one man encountering the glory of God, I believe it is a glimpse of what the believer's life should look like.

The train (visible manifestation) of Christ's robe (Kingly authority) fills the temple (heart and mind) of the believer. Every time we encounter the glory and power of our King, our hearts awaken to what He has finished through the cross and the grave. O, the victory of His resurrection!

STAY SEATED

I had the privilege of serving as a juror on a court case a couple of years ago. It was an interesting experience and it actually opened up my eyes to the revelation of Christ being our Advocate. One of the first things I realized was how still and quiet the plaintiff was. Other than testimony time, his words were only whispers to his attorney. While the lawyer labored intensely over the case, the plaintiff sat still. Never did he have to interject his own emotion nor did he have to stand up and wrestle with the court, rather he stayed calm and trusted the work of the attorney. Anytime the plaintiff had a question or something to interject, they would notify the attorney, lean in, and whisper their input. Other than the plaintiff and the lawyer, no one could hear the dialogue. And that was the whole point. The information was solely for the ears of the attorney alone. From that point, the attorney would interpret the information and relay it to the court.

We no longer have to tolerate the accusations of the enemy, nor do we need to negotiate with the enemy or stand up in the court room to plead our case. Rather, we just need to stay seated, keep our faith in our great High Priest, and let Him do the work. We don't need to scream at devils, we just need to stay leaned in and connected. We must learn to sit down, talk with our Advocate, and let Him handle it. He will bring the truth in our time of need.

There is a lot of duty when representing a case. It's fairly common knowledge that a top level attorney will do their best to get inside the case. They will look at it from different angles, interview for countless hours, and act out the strategy of the case in order to become better acquainted with it. Some would say they want to "become the case." Simply having head knowledge isn't enough for the elite attorney, they must get involved and acquainted with the story line.

This is what Jesus did for us. Stepping inside the human frame, He acquainted Himself with (and became) the case (see Isaiah 53:3 and Hebrews 4:15). Our great High Priest stepped into the story of broken humanity and became one of us, that He could feel the weight and reality of the fallen nature. He didn't stand a distance away in hopes we get it together. Rather, He split the skies and clothed Himself with the very garment of humanity, releasing us from the weight of our debt. Beloved, He knows good and well our struggles. Give them to Him today!

Prayer: *Jesus, I trust the finished work. I know it's sufficient and satisfactory. Therefore, I will stay seated as I fight the good fight of faith. Amen!*

WHO DO YOU SAY THAT I AM

11

SEALED WITH PROMISE

When discussing identity and who we are in Christ, there are several words that we need to become familiar with – inheritance, sonship, covenant, and promise. When we understand these Kingdom realities, we then have a cleaner lens to look through.

> *"In Him, you also, after listening to the message of truth, the gospel of your salvation – having also believed, you were sealed in Him with the Holy Spirit of promise, who is given as a pledge of our inheritance, with a view to the redemption of God's own possession, to the praise of His glory."* Ephesians 1:13-14 (NASB)

COVENANT AND PROMISE

The lens we are called to look through now is "covenant and promise." They are words that appear all throughout Scripture and describe our new life in Christ. As a new covenant minister, Paul used the words "promise(s)" and "covenant(s)" 17 times in Galatians and Ephesians alone. In fact, what we call "Old Testament" are actually old promises fulfilled in Christ, while the "New Testament" are new promises fulfilled in Him. Both eras are times where the Lord promised certain legal declarations and for the most part, they are two entirely different covenants.

Therefore, the New Testament isn't updated promises from the Old, rather it is an entirely new set of promises. Although we still see the old covenant fading away after Jesus' resurrection, New Testament writers were trying their best to bring the church into a new covenant reality. Their ministry was a new covenant one (see 2 Corinthians 3:6). It was the better way and in the words of the writer of Hebrews, it's a *"better covenant."*

"But now He has obtained a more excellent ministry, by as much as He is also the mediator of a better covenant, which has been enacted on better promises." Hebrews 8:6 (NASB)

The better covenant released better motivation:

We focus on the new covenant mainly because of motivation (what motivates us). Jesus was constantly dealing with motives (what motivated mankind). He would say "when you pray," don't make a big deal about it; "when you fast," don't dress like a bum; "when you give," don't toot your horn, etc. He wasn't telling His disciples to not pray (fast or give), instead He was telling them to do it with right motivation.

The old covenant was motivated by LAW. New covenant is motivated by LOVE. Jesus says, "If you love Me, you'll keep My commandments." He wasn't saying this to control us (using love as the carrot on a stick), instead He was declaring if we fell in love, works would testify of our devotion to Him. Ephesians 1:15 declares that He chose us because He was in love. His motive for setting us apart was love! (from "Exploring our Freedom in Christ")

The writer of Hebrews (a book centered around the new covenant) tells us, *"Discover creative ways to encourage others and to motivate them toward acts of compassion, doing beautiful works as expressions of love* (Hebrews 10:24)"

VARIOUS TYPES OF COVENANTS

Covenants are promises that involve two parties. Webster's Dictionary defines promise as, "A declaration that one will do or refrain from doing something specified; a legally binding declaration that gives the person to whom it is made a right to expect or to claim the performance or forbearance of a specified act." In other words, a promise is a legal declaration that the promiser will come through. It's an oath that ensures action. Can you see the promise of God revealed through the gospel? The Father promised a breakthrough of hope and peace with God, and He ensured it with action.

In the Bible, there are 5 covenants mentioned – *Noahic, Abrahamic, Mosaic, Davidic, and New Covenant*. Inside of these covenants, there are different types. The three I want to mention are *grant, kinship, and vassal* – each of the 5 covenants fall under one of the 3 types. Those types are:

Grants do not have to be paid back, only received and used for the recipients' benefit. Covenants under the grant were *Noahic* (Genesis 9:11) *Abrahamic* (Genesis 12:1-3; 22:15-18), and *Davidic* (2 Samuel 7:12-17).

Kinship is a covenant made between two equal parties, where they are making peace. If the convent is broken, the other party is eligible to relinquish their side of the covenant. Although this covenant is conditional, it usually includes no punishment.

Vassal is a treaty between unequal parties that depends on obedience to specific terms. You can think of this covenant as a conditional promise, where one of the parties (i.e. a king) is stronger than the other and able to punish if not fulfilled by the recipient. In a vassal covenant, the lesser is obligated to the greater one. Some synonyms for vassal are "servant, slave, subject." A covenant under the vassal was the *Mosaic* – the conditional covenant that required Israel's response (see Exodus 20:18-19; Deuteronomy 5:25-27).

FROM GRANT TO VASSAL COVENANT

When God led Israel out of Egypt, He extended the grant covenant, one intended for an entire nation. In fact, it mirrored the free covenant given to Abraham – one of greatness and multiplied dominion. However, the Israelites refused the offer and instead asked for a kinship covenant, one with conditions and stipulations (see Exodus 20:18-19; Deut. 5:25-27).

Out of what I believe was a wrong view of God, they refused to enter into the Father's kind offer. The covenant extended to Abraham could've been theirs, but because of their skewed view of God as master only and not a Father, they demanded a less covenant.

Only Moses, who was brought up in the palace, could fathom relating to God as a Father and a friend. The rest saw Him the way they had seen the cruel Egyptian pharaoh and slave masters. Because of their fearful slave mindset, they sacrificed relationship and asked for rules instead. Though it was not His desire, God adjusted to the Israelites' request, and rather than the whole nation coming up to have relationship, only Moses and Aaron were allowed to come up to get the rules (see Exodus 19:20-25).

They were viewing God though the lens of a master they'd just been under – Pharoah of Egypt. The "past" stood in their way of receiving the grant (an "all-inclusive") covenant that God was releasing.

Interestingly, the orphan spirit shows up here. Instead of receiving the fullness of what God intended, they asked for added stipulations – refusing to receive the free gift of God's love, and instead looking to delegate the personal responsibility of priesthood to someone else.

Since parties under kinship couldn't change covenants while both were still living, at the death of Moses, God strikes a new covenant with Joshua and company. Under new leadership, God is changing the covenant with added stipulations. Thus, beginning in Deuteronomy, we have the change of covenant of kinship to vassal – one for equal parties, to now one of greater king to lesser king. This was a downgrade of covenant and freedom!

This is why Paul is urging Galatia to remain steady in their freedom, not going back to their former master (see Galatians 5:1). They'd been given a grant covenant and were never to return to the "Pharaoh of their souls." He wanted believers to continually explore the space of freedom. Instead of downgrades, he wanted them to understand that they were wired for upgrades.

> *"Behold, days are coming," declares the Lord, "when I will make a new covenant with the house of Israel and with the house of Judah, not like the covenant which I made with their fathers in the day I took them by the hand to bring them out of the land of Egypt, My covenant which they broke, although I was a husband to them," declares the Lord. But this is the covenant which I will make with the house of Israel after those days," declares the Lord, "I will put My law within them and on their heart I will write it; and I will be their God, and they shall be My people. They will not teach again, each man his neighbor and each man his brother, saying, 'Know the Lord,' for they will all know Me, from the least of them to the greatest of them," declares the Lord, "for I will forgive their iniquity, and their sin I will remember no more."* Jeremiah 31:31-34 (NASB)

Inside the kinship and vassal covenant, the one (of equal or lesser status) who transgressed the covenant could be cut off from the covenant (called a divorce). This is what Paul writes about in Romans 7. Jesus, bearing the sin of the world, willingly took the curse of death on a tree, cancelled the old covenant, and now extends the free gift of freedom! In light of this, John 17 was a cry of covenant, where the two equal kin parties (Father and Son) are agreeing and bringing in *"those who will believe* (see John 17:10)."

> *"So Jesus is the One who has enacted a new covenant with a new relationship with God so that those who accept the invitation will receive the eternal inheritance He has*

promised to His heirs. For He died to release us from the guilt of the violations committed under the first covenant." Hebrews 9:15 (TPT)

BETWEEN THE FATHER AND SON

It's crucial to understand the covenant that was made with us (when we believed), was actually first made between the Father and Son. This is why the Father and the Son have an ark of covenant in heaven (see Revelation 11:19; Hebrews 8:2; 9:11, 24). As the Godhead made a kinship covenant, so we being in Christ, are now recipients and beneficiaries of the promise made between them.

We are one in the covenant made between the Son and the Father! Whatever Christ received when He ascended to His Father, we who believe have received the same. All things that are in Him are in the beloved, and what can be said about Him, can be said about us. In John 17:10, Jesus says, *"I ask on their behalf; I do not ask on behalf of the world, but of those whom You have given Me; for they are Yours; and all things that are Mine are Yours, and Yours are Mine; and I have been glorified in them."* It's not like Jesus ascended into heaven, only to hear that He had to leave us at the door. He couldn't, because as we believe He joins us to Himself. The reckless love of God pulled us out of the pit, brought us into Christ, and when the glorified Christ walked into the Father's abode, we walked in with Him.

The vassal covenant was based on works and keeping all the "jotted" expectations. This high bar of behavior released fear in the hearts of people, simply because the people felt they couldn't fulfill all of its (613) requirements. This left them vulnerable for judgment under the hand of a holy God – in His holy nature, He had to judge sin. In their frail and sinful state, the weight of duty left them overwhelmed and undone. This is why Jesus came to fulfill the law (see Romans 8:1-4).

When He said, *"It is finished,"* He was in part referring to the fact that He had, once and for all, fulfilled the requirement of the covenant law. In a sense, He suddenly halted the effects of the law of punishment and the fear of never being good enough. He took what we deserved so that we could receive what He deserved. Therefore, He gave us the freedom of Sonship when we received the (grant) covenant by faith (see Romans 8:15; Galatians 4:7). Now, the Father's word and affirmation, *"This is My son,"* is what continually sets us free (see Galatians 3-4).

A NEW COVENANT

Jesus brought in a new (grant) covenant, by keeping the kinship between He and the Father. Jesus, fully God, became a man and lovingly submitted Himself to the leadership of His Father (see Luke 18:19; John 5:19; 8:28; 12:49). As He willingly laid down His life and kept His Word to the Father, He was fulfilling the covenant to a thousand generations (see Romans 8:1-4).

In Luke's opening chapter, we read about the entrance of Jesus and His forerunner assistant, John the Baptist. In this context, we also see the promise of redemption and mercy being released through men and women who say "yes" to the promises.

The first recipients of these promises were John's parents, Zacharias and Elizabeth. John's name can be translated, "He has shown us mercy, God's gracious gift," while his parents' names together mean, "He who remembers the covenant (oath)." Interestingly, we have the gospel message in their names alone: "He has shown mercy by remembering His covenant." The Holy Spirit, the seal of His covenant, was sealing promise in the hearts of Zacharias, Mary, and Elizabeth – resulting in songs of promise being released over their generation. As the Lord encounters Zacharias, he begins to prophesy:

"And his father Zacharias was filled with the Holy Spirit, and prophesied..." Luke 1:67 (NASB)

"Blessed be the Lord God of Israel, for He has visited us and accomplished redemption for His people, and has raised up a horn of salvation for us in the house of David His servant – As He spoke by the mouth of His holy prophets from of old – salvation from our enemies, and from the hand of all who hate us; to show mercy toward our fathers and to remember His holy covenant, the oath which He swore to Abraham our father, to grant us that we, being rescued from the hand of our enemies, might serve Him without fear." Luke 1:68-74 (NASB)

Both covenants given to Abraham and David were grant covenants and through the mouth of a priest, God would declare, *"The oath which He swore to Abraham our father, to GRANT US that we, being rescued from the hand of our enemies, might serve Him without fear."* Luke 1:73-74 (NASB)

Did you see that? This grant covenant detailed in Luke's gospel is one that rescues us from the enemy of fear. When I read this, I can't help but ask, "What kind of fear is the Lord communicating through Zacharias? Is it the fear of heights, fear of failure, or could it be the fear of death? Well, let's look at Romans 8, where we will find one of the crowning verses related to the freedom from fear.

"And you did not receive the "spirit of religious duty," leading you back into the fear of never being good enough. But you have received the "Spirit of full acceptance," enfolding you into the family of God. And you will never feel orphaned, for as he rises up within us, our spirits join him in saying the words of tender affection, "Beloved Father!" Romans 8:15 (TPT)

The fear that Paul addresses is one "of never being good enough." The freedom we have received declares that we are fully accepted into the family of God. As we believe and trust the finished work of Christ, we now can live knowing we (in Christ) are worthy to stand before Him. In full confidence as sons and daughters of God, we can boldly and confidently approach His throne of grace in time of need (see Hebrews 4:16).

SEALED: SETTLING THE ISSUE

"In Him, you also, after listening to the message of truth, the gospel of your salvation – having also believed, you were sealed in Him with the Holy Spirit of promise, who is given as a pledge of our inheritance, with a view to the redemption of God's own possession, to the praise of His glory." Ephesians 1:13-14 (NASB)

When Paul declared we are 'sealed', he used the Greek word 'sphragizo' meaning, "To make a seal, for security from Satan." It speaks of divine security. In other words, we have been marked off as His own possession, guarded from the danger of the enemy. Once the playground of the enemy, we are now the garden of the Father's delight: *"We are coworkers with God and you are God's cultivated garden, the house He is building."* 1 Corinthians 3:9 (TPT)

Holy Spirit is the pledge (the first fruits and foretaste) of our inheritance. He gives us a heads-up of what's to come and brings us into the experience of being His "sealed ones." He has secured us like a wedding ring, with an eternal covenant and promise.

The Holy Spirit as a seal, has four implications:

- It establishes the validity or authenticity of a document or statement. It will indicate whether a document, or a signature, is real or counterfeit. Jesus was sealed (anointed) with the Holy Spirit in the Jordan when the dove descended upon Him. The Fathers approval and affirmation was the seal that kept Him secure during the wilderness. We shouldn't fear the wildernesses of life, for we are sealed with the Holy Spirit of promise.

- It is a mark of ownership and indicates that belongs to another. As someone else's property, the stranger is warded off (see John 10).

- It is used for security, and if the seal is broken, you know it has been tampered with. The Holy Spirit stands as a guard to our inner man, resisting any interior tampering.

- It is used for the sealing of someone's fate, and refers to our unchangeable destiny. Christ in us produces His vision in us, of *"glory to glory."* (see Colossians 1:27).

Sonship is the common mark of being sealed. It was Jesus who received the seal of Sonship once the dove descended on Him. It remained on Jesus and now remains on those who have believed and trusted in Jesus. Receiving the Spirit of adoption as sons wards off any tampering of the enemy (see Romans 8:15).

12

CONFORMITY: FATHER'S PROCESS

My wife and I finished building a house the first part of 2018. It was an interesting season of our life, where we (especially myself) learned some valuable and costly lessons. One of the more important lessons I learned was that it is key to follow the blueprint. Before we ever hammered the first nail or even bought the first board, the blueprint had to be finalized. My contractor made it clear that although we had a general idea of the house layout, he would not proceed until we finalized every detail of the plans. He assured me that if we didn't, it could be a potential disaster. Contractors will understand what I'm saying. Although cosmetic changes could evolve along the way, it was crucial to establish the finished layout of the house first. So, we spent several days going back and forth, to ensure that we had the blueprint the way we envisioned. This would allow us to give the sub-contractors something to work from.

STICKING TO THE PLAN

I can imagine on day one, the Father drawing up the plans of His creation. Along with the counsel of Holy Spirit and the Son, I see

Him delicately finalizing the blueprint of Their created design. After They agree on a specific design, the Father passes the blueprint to Holy Spirit, who becomes our holy sub-contractor. From this point, the Spirit's job is to work from that blueprint, sanctifying and building us up into the finished product. This process of building includes teaching us about Christ, the Father, as well as working His gifts and fruit in and through our lives.

> *"And do not be conformed to this world, but be transformed by the renewing of your mind, so that you may prove what the will of God is, that which is good and acceptable and perfect."* Romans 12:2 (NASB)

The word 'conformed' in the Greek is syschematizo meaning "Conform to the same pattern, to fashion alike." It comes from the root word syn meaning, "union, with or together" and denotes resemblance. It's where we get the word "schematic," which is "a representation of a plan or theory in the form of an outline or model." It is a diagram, model, or drawing that represents the intended form and is designed to point us to the finished product.

WORKING FROM THE FINISHED PRODUCT

When I was young, I loved putting model cars together. It was an adventure to take fragmented pieces and form them together for a finished product. Through much of my childhood, my dad was a dirt track racer, so I really enjoyed putting the race car models together. I would always put my own personal touch on the race car, making it custom and unlike any other out there. The older I got, I would actually modify the car body and add dirt track style fenders and body moldings.

I remember the finished product would always be displayed on the front of the box as well as in the assembly instructions. However, when you opened the box, all you had were fragmented pieces. What seemed to be so perfect and complete on the exterior of the box, was completely different on the inside. So, in order to see the finished product complete, I had to follow the instructions.

The Father has the perfect schematic (plan of the finished product) for your life. Determined long ago in the Father's counsel, it is the only model that Holy Spirit follows. He has no other option. Although diverse with various expressions and personalities, the plan is to make human beings in the image of Christ, empowered by the Spirit, to release the will of the Father.

When the enemy came into the garden, he was looking to alter that image and distort the Father's plans. He sought to steal perspective, kill confidence, and destroy destiny.

Therefore, we must not let the enemy or the world tell us what our schematic is. Refusing to be fashioned from the outside-in (by lies, comparison, and wrong ideas of God), we must allow the indwelling Spirit to transform us from the inside-out. We have inside information, let us use it to our advantage.

Another word for schematic is "scheme" – a large-scale systematic plan for attaining some particular object or putting an idea into effect. Both kingdoms have a schematic laid out for mankind. The Father's is to bring us into fullness of life, while the enemy's is to *"steal and kill and destroy"* (see John 10:10). In his exhortation to stay the course, Paul warns us to wage war against the schemes (and design of lies) of the enemy:

"Finally, be strong in the Lord and in His mighty power. Put on the full armor of God, so that you can take your stand against the devil's schemes." Ephesians 6:10-11 (NIV)

If the enemy can get us to agree with his schematic, he can form perspectives and strongholds in our minds that shape the way we see God, ourselves, and others. From that point, everything good and right can begin to lose its influence in our life.

However, I have good news. Holy Spirit actually works from a finished image, not our present state. As He presently sanctifies us, He does it from the vantage point of a finished product. Like the potter who shapes the clay by seeing the vase beforehand, this is how the Holy Spirit labors. Although this process seems to be a mystery, we have the best contractor in the field. He was there on day one when the plans were being drawn up, and is forever and fully capable of doing His job. He searches out these mysteries and brings us into them by *"glory to glory"* encounters.

> *"…we speak God's wisdom in a mystery, the hidden wisdom which God predestined before the ages to our glory; the wisdom which none of the rulers of this age has understood; for if they had understood it they would not have crucified the Lord of glory; but just as it is written, Things which eye has not seen and ear has not heard, and which have not entered the heart of man, all that God has prepared for those who love Him." For to us God revealed them through the Spirit; for the Spirit searches all things, even the depths of God."* 1 Corinthians 2:7-10 (NASB)

He goes on to say…

> *"Now we have received, not the spirit of the world, but the Spirit who is from God, so that we may know the things freely given to us by God, which things we also speak, not in words taught by human wisdom, but in those taught by the Spirit, combining spiritual thoughts with spiritual words."* 1 Corinthians 2:12-13 (NASB)

It is Holy Spirit's supreme joy to bring honor and attention to the Son, thus revealing the image of who we are being formed into. In other words, He gives us vision for the finished product, by showing us who we are becoming. He places Christ before the theater screen of our soul, revealing the beauty of Who we are growing into. From this basis of honoring and adoring the beloved Son, He works day and night to conform us into that same image, from *"glory to glory"* (see 1 Corinthians 3:18).

PLANS AND PURPOSES

I sit down in the driver's seat, type in the address of the destination, and away I go. I can hardly wait to arrive at the venue. As we make our way to the designated location, I hear the GPS lady say, "Rerouting... rerouting..." What?! I'm thinking, did I miss a turn? Did I fail to hear the GPS instructions along the way? What happened that we have to re-route? Looking down at my phone, I notice that the course of action has changed. What was once a route on the main highway, I am now being directed another way. Apparently I missed instruction from the GPS but within a few seconds, I was back on track – all with a changed route plan. The destination hadn't changed, only the steps to get there. Within a few hours, I arrive at my destination, realizing that the reroute wasn't a big deal.

How many times do we miss a turn, or take an alternate step to walking out our destiny and purpose? If you're like me, you may be up into the triple digits. Sometimes I've felt like a wandering Israelite, going round and round in circles. But, thank God for His mercy! A few years ago, the Lord began to teach me the difference between purpose and plans. Although they are closely related, they're not the same – they're distinctly different. Understanding the difference will help us remain encouraged and focused in the process.

Purpose is related to our destiny, the end goal of our life. This is the part that the Father is fixed on and working from. In other words, it's the image on the front of the box – the finished product. However, plans are a little different. They are related to our process – the journey that leads to our destination. It is much like the instructions that come in the box. The steps along the way obviously have a huge part to play in our purpose. However, a sudden missed turn or failure to read signs along the way doesn't mean there isn't an alternate route. It's not like the GPS shuts down and refuses to communicate when we miss the route. Instead, there is always a route of recovery. Believe me, I know. I've taken the alternate route many times. Nonetheless, I'm thankful that He didn't give up on me, but rerouted and changed the plan.

I guess you could say that the Father is more focused on the purpose (finished product) than the plans (instructions along the way). In other words, He is okay with you missing a turn as long as you don't forfeit the destination. As the One committed to our journey, He is watching our steps and is faithful to see us through.

"There has never been the slightest doubt in my mind that the God who started this great work in you would keep at it and bring it to a flourishing finish on the very day Christ Jesus appears." Philippians 1:6 (The Message)

THE INNER GPS

I know there have been several times where I've ignored the (GPS) "gut-check," only to look back and see that I missed the sign given on my route. I could very well be standing in the midst of a particular destination, only to look back and see some failed attempts. That's when I throw my hands up and thank God for His mercy – those moments where He rerouted my journey. Thank heaven that He didn't stop the car, open the door, and throw me out…no, He simply notified me that we were changing some steps in getting there.

With that said, the Lord has predesigned our destiny (purpose). He has something so glorious in mind. In fact, it's much more than we could ever imagine or think. So, to accomplish these feats, He hardwires us with an inner GPS, the Holy Spirit. From that point, the (indwelling) Spirit constantly interacts with our soul (mind, will, emotions) to guide us in route – communicating with the satellite systems to ensure we have the most expedient and beneficial course of action. Jesus declares that the Spirit will communicate what He hears from the heavenly satellite system, only to then relay that message to the beloved. Along the way, we may experience failed attempts to follow the instruction, yet as we yield to the inner voice, He will bring us back onto the course of action. This is the "Spirit-led" life.

> *"But when He, the Spirit of truth comes, He will guide you into all the truth; for He will not speak on His own initiative, but whatever He hears, He will speak; and He will disclose to you what is to come."* John 16:13 (NASB)

Many times, we can get lost on the way, simply because we can't see the specified route. It's easy to look around and see everyone else's journey, thinking ours should look similar. Although there are definite foundational (Biblical) principles we should all apply to our lives, our personal journeys' all look different. They vary from one believer to another. When we try to "copy and paste" each others' journey, we miss the unique dealings of the Lord in our own lives.

REFUSING TO COMPARE

Therefore, the Father is not concerned about comparison. Instead, He is passionate about conformity. When we compare ourselves to others (i.e. talents, abilities, and gifts), we miss out on the glorious process of conformity (into the image of Christ). We were never called to be someone else, nor do we possess the grace needed to carry their calling. Friends, we were designed to carry our own destiny in Him. When we try to bear the image of someone else, we open the door to all kinds of weirdness. It's just not the way we are supposed to walk.

In building the house of prayer from the ground up, I've personally experienced the temptation to be like other ministries and adopt the same things they are doing. It was real strong in the early days, around 2011-2012. Trying to establish something effective and fruitful, I sometimes thought it might be most beneficial to mold my expression to look like others. However, in 2012, the Lord began to release a fresh grace to see the uniqueness of what we were building at One27 House of Prayer. Through several personal encounters concerning identity and a handful of prophetic words, the Lord began to chip away at the mindset of comparing what we had to other ministries. Instead, He released a confidence that we were building something that was needed in the Kingdom.

WEAR YOUR OWN ARMOR

David was confronted with an important decision when facing Goliath. Among the many threats coming at him, the temptation of comparison was definitely at the top – and it started right from the beginning. Saul had always relied on his own armor and thus tried to place it on David: *"Then Saul dressed David in his own tunic. He put a coat of armor on him and a bronze helmet on his head. David fastened on his sword over the tunic and tried walking around, because he was not used to them."* 1 Samuel 17:38-39 (NIV)

To the religious, it's always easier doing things the way they've always been done. However, David as a fierce, creative worshipper says to Saul, *"I cannot go in these… because I am not used to them. So he took them off. Then he took his staff in his hand, chose five smooth stones from the stream, put them in the pouch of his shepherd's bag and, with his sling in his hand, approached the Philistine"* (1 Samuel 17:39-40). In his unique battle style, David steps on the scene with an undivided heart and unwavering focus to defeat anything that hindered God's name from going forth. He couldn't rely on the way things had been done before, instead he leaned into what the Lord had uniquely placed inside of him. Let us understand, we're always more powerful and protected in our uniqueness, than we are in someone else's.

"We were designed with the capacity to be conformed into the likeness of Jesus, the One resurrected from the dead, seated at the right hand of the Father." -Bill Johnson

13

COMPARISON: IDENTITY'S NEMESIS

"Make a careful exploration of who you are and the work you have been given, and then sink yourself into that. Don't be impressed with yourself. Don't compare yourself with others. Each of you must take responsibility for doing the creative best you can with your own life." Galatians 6:4 (The Message)

One of the biggest temptations in the body of Christ is comparison. It comes in various forms such as comparing self-image, money, careers, stats, and so on. The most common of comparisons is when we compare our journey to someone else's. Many times these comparisons are in the context of identity issues – not feeling like our life or ministry matters. This usually enters in when we feel we must attain a certain spiritual status to really be significant. What's interesting is, envy (the desire to have a quality, possession, or other desirable attribute belonging to someone else) is at the heart of this.

Although we need people in our lives to encourage and equip us in our walk with the Lord, we were never supposed to be them. Everyone has their own identity and journey to tell a panoramic story of who God is. This is why God never made just one color. He knew that white wouldn't express His full personality, nor would trees be the only creation to declare His praise – He went on to make a full expansion of His creative wisdom. He wanted endless expressions (such as colors and sounds) to minister to Him.

The beauty of various colors, objects, and people in the Bible reveal the Person of Christ. They each serve their divine purpose as they point to Him. For example, the color red signified the coming washing of the blood of the Lamb. Violet used in the Tabernacle would signify the royalty of the King of kings. The brazen laver represented the washing of the water of the Word. I think you get the idea.

Therefore, we see that comparison is not from God. It is straight from the enemy, and he uses it to suppress the identity and calling of the saints. He knows if he can get us second guessing who we are, he can get our eyes off of the prize. Discipleship and mentorship is from the Lord, but comparison is not. As Bob Sorge says, "Discipleship is when we learn faith, not necessarily the conduct".

Theodore Roosevelt once said that "Comparison is the thief of joy." It lays siege on your soul. Our tendency to compare (envy) is so fundamental to our fallen identity that God chose to address it from the start in the 10 commandments (see Exodus 10:17).

THE DANGER OF COMPARISON

One of Israel's grave mistakes was in their desire to be like other nations. From the basis of comparison, she cried out for a king (see 1 Samuel 8:19-22). Although Israel was destined to have Yahweh as their presiding king, this call was forfeited by selfish ambition and the envy of other nations. God was calling them into a unique leadership style, but they just couldn't look past the way things had been done around them. In the same way, I believe that envy and comparison are among the fiercest opponents of our identity in Christ.

"For it is not he who commends himself that is approved, but he whom the Lord commends." 2 Corinthians 10:18 (NASB)

The Message translation says it this way, *"It's what God says about you that makes the difference."*

Comparing ourselves to one another is an easy trap to fall into, seeing that our culture is driven by outward image and the pursuit of happiness. The world tells us to measure our lives in proportion to what others have or what they enjoy, which is why we are usually tempted to buy bigger, better, and brighter.

Comparison is dangerous because:

- It questions God's nature and His great creative power. We are actually agreeing with satan when we question who we are.

- It stifles our identity in Christ. Nothing creates a fog in the minds of people more than when they measure their walk with someone else. Our walk is to be measured by one Man, Christ. He is the image we are conforming into (see Romans 12:1-2).

- It creates unreal pictures about others, resulting in unhealthy competition. Comparison is the essence of pride and ultimately stirs up a jealous spirit.

- It disrupts unity and peace, by fostering disorder and strife. In other words, comparison wars against creativity and community (see James 3:16).

When Israel desired to be "anything but that" and demanded a king *"like the other nations,"* they received Saul as their leader. What began as a desire soon became their own dismay. God made it clear to Samuel, *"They have rejected Me as their King, not you as their prophet* (see 1 Samuel 8:7)." This gross substitution was birthed from the foul stench of comparison.

"Comparison is one of the greatest enemies of the anointing" -John Grey

A NEW GRADING SYSTEM

The Lord came with a different grading system. Just like He did with David, He measures us according to our heart, not to outward abilities.

"But God told Samuel, "Looks aren't everything. Don't be impressed with his looks and stature. I've already eliminated him. God judges persons differently than humans do. Men and women look at the face; God looks into the heart." 1 Samuel 16:7 (The Message)

God sets the record straight through Samuel, and declares his mission statement for coming kings. Saul represents the flesh (acts of comparison), David represents the Spirit (of resting in the Lord). While Saul was cultivating the exterior and coddling the opinions of men, David was tending a fiery heart. Focused on the interior, David knew that heaven was watching and positioned himself accordingly. This put him in great standing with the Lord, which ultimately translated to favor with those around him.

Once David began to step into the favor of influence on his life, Saul and his envious heart of comparison surfaced. While the women of Israel acknowledged and praised David for slaying tens of thousands, Saul sought to slay the young man. Instead of Saul seeing the opportunity as a compliment to his kingdom and leadership, he finds David to be a threat. What if Saul would've been secure in who he was? Could you imagine what it would've looked like if Saul could've slain his flesh instead, choosing to honor and prefer those coming up in the ranks? Isn't that what true fathers do, preferring their sons above themselves?

EMBRACING UNIQUENESS

The Lord's message to humanity's uniqueness can be found in our bodies. Everyone has a unique fingerprint, skin pigmentation, and even birth marks. Of these, I am most fascinated with the fingerprint – the mark on our lives that is more unique than our DNA. Interestingly, no two are the same. In fact, even though identical twins share the same DNA, they will never have the same fingerprint. It's been said that there is a one in 60 billion chance that our fingerprint will match up with someone else's.

Currently, there are approximately 7 billion people alive in the world right now. Let me write that number out...7,000,000,000! This means we would have to wait and tally up 8 generations to even see if there was a match to you. Let that sink in...there is no way for anyone out there to have the same fingerprint as you. How cool is that!

Scientific studies show that fingerprints (patterns known as whorls, valleys, and ridges on the finger) are formed by maternal pressure, while in the mother's womb. Even though our bodily appearance changes, our fingerprints never change. I think it's awesome that when Yahweh formed man from the dust, He left His fingerprint on us. In other words, the original Artist made the only one out there. I've heard it said, "When you were made, they threw away the mold." The same could be said about us, His delighted in creation. He did this so we could bring a specific aspect of His nature to the table. When He formed us in our mother's womb, He indeed tossed the mold.

> *"You formed my innermost being, shaping my delicate inside and my intricate outside, and wove them all together in my mother's womb. I thank You God, for making me so mysteriously complex! Everything you do is marvelously breathtaking! It simply amazes me to think about it! How thoroughly you know me, Lord! You even shaped every bone in my body, when You created me in the secret place, carefully, skillfully shaping me from nothing to something! You saw who You created me to be, before I*

became me! Before I'd ever seen the light of day, the number of days You planned for me, were all recorded in Your book." Psalm 139:13-16 (TPT)

One of the most powerful dynamics of lifting our hands in praise is, we are extending and offering our uniqueness to God. In other words, as we extend our fingerprints, we are offering our unique stamp of approval to Him in loving adoration. This is why no two "praisers" are the same. In fact, no two songs are the same. Think about it…there are only 12 notes in music, yet we are continually producing new sounds and composing new songs. What one generation heard will be different than what the previous did. In light of this, I think it's interesting that the Lord raised up 12 unique tribes and 12 diverse disciples to represent Him and to establish His Kingdom on earth. The song locked up in each of their lives' would be what He longed to bring forth. Being diversely different, they carried something that the other was missing in the grander scheme of things. As my brother Ryan would say, "Diversity isn't a curse, it's God's gift to us."

"In the same way, I tell you, there is joy in the presence of the angels of God over one sinner who repents." Luke 15:10 (NASB)

I think it's quite amazing that the angles rejoice when one gets saved. Think about it, heaven throws a party when one part of creation gets redeemed. Perhaps this is because a new and unique song is entering the realm of heaven. In other words, the hosts of heaven (seraphim, cherubim, four living creatures and 24 elders) get a new singing partner. Heaven gets more intense in sound when a soul enters through the door. Therefore, God desires to bring your melody into the fellowship of the angels. Heaven is after your song.

"The heart that has been changed by the gospel sings the praise of the Savior… He is our new song." -John Piper

ENVY, JEALOUSY, AND STRIFE

One of the clearest expressions of comparison is in the form of envy. As we see in the account of Cain and Abel, envy reared its ugly head early on in the game. Its one of the ancient tools of the enemy, and I've heard it said that envy is, "The most underrated sin in satan's arsenal."

"Envy is often rooted in a struggle to gain identity." -Bob Sorge

Merriam Webster defines envy as "A painful or resentful awareness of an advantage enjoyed by another joined with a desire to possess the same advantage." This is why I believe it is one of the most potent killers of joy. I've personally seen the effects of it in my own personal life – not to mention how I've seen the effects of it in church (family) life. It ushers in all forms of evil.

"For where you have envy and selfish ambition, there you find disorder and every evil practice." James 3:16 (**NIV**)

The story of Saul and David reveals how even those with an exterior title of "king" can often be mere slaves inside. When the enemies of Israel were being subdued under the leadership of David, we see that Saul soon became envious and ultimately jealous. Instead of being a (sort of) father to David, he instead allows rage to fill his heart. While David should've been a recipient of Saul's blessing, he soon becomes a target of his wrath. The torment of envy drove his flesh to pursue David through the landscape of Israel and what should've been a glorious display of honor and legacy, becomes nothing more than a wide-open spectacle of flesh-dominated leadership. Talk about missing your moment!

In the life of Saul, we see that two of the four intolerable things are fulfilled:

"(When) a slave becomes a king, (and) an overbearing fool who prospers..." Proverbs 30:22 (NLT)

REVEALING HEARTS

When Jesus wanted to reveal the hidden sin of envy in the hearts of men, He told the parable of the landowner (see Matthew 20:1-16). Jesus had a way of bringing his listeners into another world of thought and with this one, He tells of a master who rewarded all of his laborers with the same wage. Yep, even though their times of hire were different, the master rewarded them all the same. In other words, even though their date of employment was all over the board, pay was identical. Just imagine how you would feel if you went to pick up your paycheck on payday, and learned that someone with less credentials or a later hire date received the same amount that you did. It would be pretty hard to swallow, wouldn't it?

Again, when Jesus told this parable, He wanted to communicate a critical issue among His disciples. The idea that Jesus wanted to bring attention to was this – the Father knows how and who to reward. Although the circumstances (and favor) don't always make sense, He just wants us to trust Him – all while rejoicing in whatever gift we or our brothers and sisters receive. Let's look at what Jesus says:

> *"Those hired at five o'clock came up and were each given a dollar. When those who were hired first saw that, they assumed they would get far more. But they got the same, each of them one dollar. Taking the dollar, they groused angrily to the manager, 'These last workers put in only one easy hour, and you just made them equal to us, who slaved all day under a scorching sun.'* Matthew 20:9-12 (The Message)

Interestingly, the workers' hearts were revealed on payday and as the master's steward shelled out the cash, they spilled their opinions about the matter. What was in their heart soon came out of their mouths. I like how Bill Johnson says, "God will often offend the mind to reveal the heart." That is most definitely true in this case, as the servants could not wrap their finite minds around the fact that lesser work still meant equal pay. In essence, their minds were offended by this "unreasonable act."

COMPARISON: IDENTITY'S NEMESIS

Remember, it was James (Jesus' brother) who wrote, *"For where you have envy and selfish ambition, there you find disorder and every evil practice* (James 3:16 NIV)." I'm pretty sure James was familiar with the emotion of envy. Can you imagine what it was like being Jesus's brother? I mean, the Creator of the universe (through whom all things were made) is your sibling.

I can just imagine that secretly Jesus was the favorite. He made the best grades, had endless wisdom, and could speak with such clarity and conviction. Think about it, at age 12, He was in the temple, blowing minds with heavenly wisdom – even the scribes (professional writers) couldn't comprehend the truths He spoke. Not to mention, later, He was calming the waves, feeding the masses, and raising the dead. I think it would be safe to say that it was probably awkward growing up with the Prince of Peace as your brother, and if anyone felt the weight of envy and the clinches of comparison, it would've been James. Praise God, James passed the test!

He goes on to write that envy opens up the door to every evil thing. I like what Kris Vallotton says, "James warns us that what is initiated as a struggle in our hearts eventually gives place to demonic spirits that wreak havoc on the very core of our being." That's pretty intense! How could it be that one sin could have such a widespread effect? I personally believe that envy reveals a deeper level of frailty – our lack of trust in the Lord. It shows we are not willing to give Him Lordship over certain areas. It has been said that trust is the heart of relationship. If that is the case, when we envy and strive with one another, we are slowing down the heart.

IT'S A SIBLING THING

It's interesting that throughout Scripture, contention and striving between brothers is prevalent. From the first account of Cain and Abel, to the bout between Esau and Jacob, envy among male siblings is a recurring situation. Furthermore, we see that brothers aren't the only ones susceptible to the temptation of envy. I like what Bob Sorge says:

"It wasn't only His brothers who envied Jesus. The religious leaders of His day envied Him intensely because they viewed Him as a competitor in their sphere. Jesus' public ministry was a constant dance of His regulating the temperature of envy in the hearts of the religious leaders. If their envy got too hot too soon, they would crucify Him prematurely." (from 'Envy: The Enemy Within' by Bob Sorge)

As we see in the lives of Sarah and Hagar, women also had their fair share of giving host to the temptation of envy. Sarah was promised a child in her latter years, and while losing hope in the promise, she chose to give the responsibility to Hagar her maidservant.

"Now Sarai, Abram's wife had borne him no children, and she had an Egyptian maid whose name was Hagar. So Sarai said to Abram, 'Now behold, the Lord has prevented me from bearing children. Please go in to my maid; perhaps I will obtain children through her.' And Abram listened to the voice of Sarai." Genesis 16:1-2 (NASB)

Instead of trusting and waiting on the Lord, she delegated her promise to someone else. What was meant for Sarah was soon passed to Hagar. It was in the Lord's plan to bring about a child through Sarah, but taking the alternate route, she opened up the door for the enemy to bring bondage – even on down to generations following her. Soon, it was envy and jealousy that caused Ishmael to mock Isaac. What began with Sarah was soon perpetuated into the life of the next generation. In other words, the subtle entry of envy opened the door to "disorder and every evil practice." This shows us that the Lord desires to bring about pure promise in our lives, free of envy and comparison. When I envy someone else's journey, I distort my personal process and invite other evils that I was never intended to fight.

Might I even suggest that comparison and envy are two primary evils in the enemy's tool belt? In fact, these companion evils were at the heart of satan's fall, for he said, *"I will be like God* (Isaiah 14:14)." Instead of embracing his destiny as an angelic being created for worship, he allowed envy, jealousy, and contention to drive him into madness – he reached for something that was outside of his jurisdiction. If it's true that wounded people are the ones who wound people, satan has to be the most wounded individual in the universe. Just as he has suffered, he wants to bring you and I into a wounded state of pain and failed destiny.

Comparison and envy are two components of evil that long to strip us of our inheritance as sons and daughters. Comparison will mock, envy will accuse, and both will ultimately weaken our resolve to abide in Him – and unless we resist, they will steal our focus away from Jesus, the great image. Therefore, let us cast off the burden of these two evils and live out who we are in Him. Let us awaken and realize that we don't have the grace to live in someone else's destiny. Simply said, let us be us – the individuals He has called us to be.

I was never given the vision to live inside someone else's world, nor was I called to their journey. I am called to cultivate my own garden and no one else's. Yes, I can be a part of their journey, but at the end of the day, I am responsible for my own heart posture. Jesus said, *"Love the Lord your God"* He didn't say, "Make sure your neighbor is loving." Holy Spirit produces in us the fruit of self-control, not others-control.

PREFERENCE IN THE EARLY CHURCH

In Acts 1, Jesus' senior leadership team was needing a 12th member and the decision came down to the choice between Matthias and Joseph. I'm sure it was an intense moment, as the fate of the twelve would be decided with a mere drawing of lots. As Scripture tells us, Matthias would advance to the Lord's senior leadership team – kinda reminds me of the time we used to play basketball during school recess, and the teams were hand-picked.

You would always stand with that awkward look on your face, hoping that you weren't the last one picked. Yeah, that was always an intense moment.

I'm sure glad that Joseph kept his cool and remained mature when Matthias ended up being the chosen one. I may be reading into this a bit, but I can't help but believe that Joseph's response of trusting in the Lord paved the way for them to be *"in one place"* (see Acts 2:11). Perhaps it was a choice that would resound throughout the early church. In light of this, we must understand that envy and jealousy not only wage war on our identity, but also the family of God. When we allow these foul evils to penetrate our lives, we are creating a bigger mess than just the present. Today's compromise can become a large battle for those following. In light of this, may we give ourselves to preferring and honoring one another with such humility and patience. It is the better way!

We can in no way customize our destiny, for Scripture makes it clear that God is the One who ordains our steps; our life is in His hands (see Psalm 37:23). Although the Lord never controls us, He is highly involved in leading us. It's just what He does, and He does it so well. As sons and daughters of the King, we must never measure our success by the size of our ministries, by the amount of influence in our lives, or the size of our bank account. Those things are important, just not primary or first place. Rather, we must measure our stature and success by what He says about us and how He sees us. (from "Equip: Raising Up a Mature Body")

PREPARATION AND PURPOSE

As we pursue uniqueness and identity, I believe it's important to understand the difference between preparation and purpose. Although the preparation of believers may look the same, the purpose will always be different. In other words, I strongly believe that there are some essential values to cultivating life in God that every believer should be adopting into into their walk. Some of those core values would be a lifestyle of prayer, fasting, devotion to His word, and belonging to a positive community of believers. These are non-negotiable in the Kingdom of God.

Think about it this way – most bull riders will stretch out extensively before they jump on their bull of choice. They'll put their leg up on the fence and stretch like a ballerina or gymnast. This is to prepare for their few seconds of being thrown around. Although the stretching is crucial, it doesn't make them a gymnast or ballerina. They may have similar preparations, but when it comes down to it, gymnasts and bull riders are two totally different callings. Could you see the bull rider jumping on a balance bar, or could you see a ballerina jumping on a wild bull. Absolutely not! Yes, their preparation looks similar, but their job has totally different dynamics. Same goes for us – although there are core values that we all need to adopt into our walk with Jesus, it doesn't make us the same. We are one body with many functions and expressions. Let your expression be heard!

> *"Just as the human body is one, though it has many parts that together form one body, so too is Christ. For by one Spirit we all were immersed and mingled into one single body. And no matter our status—whether we are Jews or non-Jews, oppressed or free – we are all privileged to drink deeply of the same Holy Spirit."* 1 Corinthians 12:12-13 (TPT)

WHO DO YOU SAY THAT I AM

14

TEARING DOWN STRUCTURES

As I stated earlier, my wife and I finished building a house last year and might I add, we learned a lot! It was one interesting 6 months of our lives to say the least. Among the many things I learned during the construction, there is one lesson I will never forget – a right foundation is absolutely necessary. I have somewhat understood this truth throughout my life, but it really came to life when we embarked on the house-building journey. To save you from unnecessary details, let's just say we had some faulty framers on the front end – it was obvious they weren't the sharpest tools in the shed, so we had to let them go.

After a careful search, we hired our second framer. Thinking he was a good builder, we soon found out otherwise. In fact, he was almost as bad as the first and ended up making a bigger mess. This thing was going south quickly and I found myself saying, "I have no business building a house." However, after two failed attempts, we finally landed a competent builder. I knew that he had his work cut out.

So, to survey the damages and to get a game plan of moving forward, we met with the new builder. After a careful inquiry and survey of the previous builder's work, he made it clear that we had some foundation issues.

It would require a few days of fixing the issues before he could move forward with building the walls. He walked me around the perimeter of the house walls, showing me how a faulty foundation would affect him moving forward. At a distance, I hardly noticed the damage, but as he pointed them out closely, I could definitely see we had caught this just in time. After an hour or so, he assured me that he could fix the issues. Although I was a bit disappointed with the current work, I was also grateful that we had found someone who could finish the job correctly.

As I drove away from the construction site that day, a simple but profound truth come to life to me – if the foundation isn't square and in alignment with the original plan, the rest of the house just won't be right. Although we could've stacked some walls on the existing foundation, over time the imperfection would become more and more evident. Storms and seasons of life would soon reveal what laid beneath. We could've neglected and ignored the current foundation issues at hand, however as time went by, those internal problems would soon surface.

I say all of that to say this – sometimes we focus on the exterior walls of our lives when in fact, the foundation is the part that needs the most attention. What lays beneath is the most important, and if we are carrying any faulty perspectives in our hearts towards God or ourselves, the exterior of our lives just won't function properly. We can dress up our lives with neat behavior, but eventually, the walls will show the unseen. Therefore, we must allow the Holy Spirit to plumb line the foundation of our lives, uprooting anything that does not line up with His heart and mind.

> *"We are destroying speculations and every lofty thing raised up against the knowledge of God, and we are taking every thought captive to the obedience of Christ, and we are ready to punish all disobedience, whenever your obedience is complete."* 2 Corinthians 10:5 (NASB)

FOUNDATIONS OF THOUGHT

When I talk about foundations, I am mostly referring to mindsets (and thought patterns) on which our lives rest. They determine how we respond to the Lord. With that being said, I believe it's crucial to understand how the Lord works with our minds to bring transformation in our lives. We can either believe unto behaving, or we can behave unto believing. See more below:

Kingdom of God method of transformation is *believe unto behaving*.

If the Lord can "convince" us of who He is and who He is in us, the impossibilities become possible. Therefore, the Holy Spirit will always seek to build your belief (faith) before He improves your behavior. This (believing unto behaving) is the "inside-out" reality.

For example, let's say there's a sincere believer who loves Jesus. One night, they're out a little too late and end up having too much to drink. This leads to other sinful acts that spin out of control. Shortly after, out of sincere remorse, they repent and cry out to God for help in their weakness. At that point, it's as if it never happened. The Lord then works to convince them they are the righteousness of God in Christ, thus building them up from the inside-out.

In addition to the myriad of Scriptures we have to convince us of our old life being crucified, He gives us the Holy Spirit, our inner instructor who constantly reminds us of who we are – that we belong to Him and are forever in His family. If the Holy Spirit can move us into believing and receiving our identity in Christ, He can remove any conflicting mindsets that may reside in our soul.

Therefore, understanding our position in Christ spurs us on to godly living in this age. Peter calls this, *"promises that enable you…"* (see 2 Peter 1:4 NLT)

The enemy's method of transformation is *behaving unto believing*.

In the same situation with the sincere believer, unfortunately there is one who hasn't forgotten – his name is the accuser (satan). From the moment the sin is committed, the enemy works to remind them of how bad they are. In other words, he wants that believer to identify with the act of what they did. If the enemy can cause us to put our faith in what we do rather than who we are, he can create a swirl of confusion, rather than clarity.

If the enemy can "convince" us that we are defined by our behavior, he can weaken our identity. This (behaving unto believing) is the "outside-in" reality.

Let's take this a step further and look at how the enemy forms beliefs that ultimately affect our behavior. Satan takes the thoughts and feelings we receive into our (sub)conscious, infuses the information with his interpretation, and craftily forms them into belief systems. He works to remind us again and again of these occurrences and distorts them with his interpretations to the point that we accept his suggestions as truth. These subtle lies then become a part of our belief system, which explains why something that occurs years and even decades ago, can affect and even steer our life.

What happens to us (the facts and events) is not really what creates a stronghold. What we believe about it is what creates a stronghold. This is why similar circumstances can derail one person, while motivating another. In other words, the same circumstance with opposing beliefs will always have different outcomes.

CORNERSTONES OF OUR FAITH

I have identified 3 foundational elements of our identity – what God says about God, what God says about us, and what God says is available. When there is a breakdown of these 3 foundational truths, the house becomes faulty and misaligned. However, as cornerstones to our faith, I believe embracing these through a Biblical lens will lead us into a life of perpetual victory and breakthrough.

What God says about God

Throughout the Word of God, we have direct statements from Yahweh about Himself. In fact, the recurring statement concerning the children of Israel's freedom was one founded on Yahweh's identity. In Exodus 6:6, He says, *"Say, therefore, to the sons of Israel, 'I AM the LORD, and I will bring you out from under the burdens of the Egyptians, and I will deliver you from their bondage. I will also redeem you with an outstretched arm and with great judgments."* In other words, the freedom that Israel desired, came in understanding who He was as their Lord.

Although Exodus 6 is a specific passage about God leading the Israelites out, it also speaks of what He does for us as we put our trust in Him – He brings us out, redeems us, and through our lives, He releases His judgments against darkness. He does all these things out of His nature. He moves simply because He is good! In other words, "I WILL" proceeds from "I AM."

Prayer: *Father, I believe Jesus represented you to the fullest account. What I see in His life, I see in Your heart. Although I am learning and increasing in the knowledge of God, I repent for any negative thoughts I have about You. I ask that You would fill me with the knowledge of Your Son and open my eyes to see You more clearly. I renounce any mindsets that resist the knowledge of God and I receive freedom to live aware of Your nature. In Jesus' name!*

What God says about us

No matter what others may say, His Word is the one opinion that stands the test of time. He has the final say, and posturing our hearts to receive what He declares over us is key. Let me just throw some Scriptures out there, and let them do the talking.

The Father makes it clear what the Son accomplished on our behalf, *"He made Him who knew no sin to be sin on our behalf, so that we might become the righteousness of God in Him."* 2 Corinthians 5:21 (NASB)

Maybe there are times you feel like an orphan, casted away and left alone. It's time to leave that emotion behind, for He declares over you, *"To all who believed him and accepted him, he gave the right to become children of God."* John 1:12 (NLT)

I know you may feel overlooked, but He says you are His treasure, and you are valuable: *"You are God's chosen treasure—priests who are kings, a spiritual "nation" set apart as God's devoted ones. He called you out of darkness to experience his marvelous light, and now he claims you as his very own. He did this so that you would broadcast his glorious wonders throughout the world. For at one time you were not God's people, but now you are. At one time you knew nothing of God's mercy, because you hadn't received it yet, but now you are drenched with it!"* 1 Peter 2:9-10 (TPT)

I know the enemy says, "If you'd just get your stuff together, you'd be accepted." The Father has a different word: *"In Him you have been made complete, and He is the head over all rule and authority…"* Colossians 2:10 (NASB)

What God says is available

When Jesus came to the earth, He set before us the realm of impossibilities, only to be accomplished in the arena of trust and dependency. One of the clearest statements made by Jesus as to what is available is in John 14:12 saying, *"I tell you this timeless truth: The person who follows Me in faith, believing in Me, will do the same mighty miracles that I do – even greater miracles than these because I go to be with My Father* (TPT)." I have studied the word *"greater"* and you won't believe what it means. In the Greek language, it is the word "meizon" and yes, it means "greater." Some things in the Bible just mean what they say and say what they mean. This is one of these super-simplistic statements that Jesus made, yet because it is dangerous to the kingdom of darkness, religion seeks to play it down.

I find it interesting that before He was resurrected or would send the Holy Spirit, Jesus sent out 70 disciples to heal the sick, raise the dead, cleanse the lepers, and cast out devils. He gave them authority and power to represent who He was and what He did. In other words, His leadership team was commissioned to do the stuff. Luke 9:1 says, *"Jesus summoned together His twelve apostles, and imparted to them authority over every demon and the power to heal every disease* (TPT)." Note: Authority speaks of the nature of Jesus while power signifies the deeds of Jesus. So, let me ask you, If Jesus' disciples could do the stuff before Jesus ever rose from the dead and put His Spirit upon them, what do you think we can do? Think about it!

> *"And if the Spirit of him who raised Jesus from the dead is living in you, he who raised Christ from the dead will also give life to your mortal bodies because of his Spirit who lives in you."* Romans 8:11 (NIV)

Friends, we live in a Kingdom where momentum is increasing. The word of a ruling King and His unending Kingdom has already gone viral. The prophet Isaiah declared, *"There will be no end to the increase of His government or of peace* (Isaiah 9:7)." This Kingdom belongs to a Man at rest, sitting on a throne that is standing. In the strongest of storms and the mightiest of persecution, the Kingdom is going forth in power and He has a people who will *"Volunteer freely in the day of His power* (Psalm 110:3a)."

Will you be part of that prophetic promise? The apostle Peter says in 2 Peter 1:3-4, *"Seeing that His divine power has granted to us everything pertaining to life and godliness, through the true knowledge of Him who called us by His own glory and excellence. For by these He has granted to us His precious and magnificent promises, so that by them you may become partakers of the divine nature, having escaped the corruption that is in the world by lust."*

We have been given everything pertaining to life and godliness. This is good news! Will you jump in with both feet and enjoy the benefits of being a child in the Kingdom? It pays great dividends!

PURITY AND POSTURE

It's interesting that Jesus released His identity to the woman at the well (see John 4) before He did to the disciples (Matthew 16). One can't help but see the eagerness of Jesus to show her who He was, for it wasn't long into the conversation, when Jesus began saying, *"If you only knew who was standing in front of you, you would ask Me for living water."* In other words, He was practically waving His arms in the air, saying, "Come on, just ask me for living water, I dare you!" Perhaps He did this because of her humble heart, for a pure and contrite heart He cannot deny. Although the lady had several issues that He was about to tenderly confront, Jesus couldn't help but find Himself drawn to the posture of her broken heart. As we continue to see throughout Scripture, purity is always the perfect environment for God to release the right revelation needed in the moment. Purity gives Him access to our hearts – it's the "green light" for God to come right on in to our souls and make His abode.

Thus says the Lord, "Heaven is My throne and the earth is My footstool. Where then is a house you could build for Me? And where is a place that I may rest? For My hand made all these things, thus all these things came into being," declares the Lord. "But to this one I will look, to him who is humble and contrite of spirit, and who trembles at My word." Isaiah 66:1-2 (NASB)

DETHRONING SHAME

One of the detriments of sin and disobedience is the result of shame. It wars against our posture and purity. While guilt is related to what we've done, shame attacks who we are. Just like it did with Adam and Eve, shame causes us to hide from the presence of the Lord.

"They heard the sound of the Lord God walking in the garden in the cool of the day, and the man and his wife hid themselves from the presence of the Lord God among the trees of the garden." Genesis 3:8 (NASB)

Just like Adam and Eve before the fall, we as human beings, are called to live totally free before the Lord. In fact, it is for freedom that Christ set us free (see Galatians 5:1). Jesus' first miracle was turning the water into wine, in order to remove shame from the bridegroom (as he failed to supply the wedding with enough wine). He died and rose so we would be severed from the shame and condemnation that Adam and Eve encountered.

Free from fear and timidity, we were made to walk with confidence in the *"cool of the day"* with God. However, any time we listen to the voice of shame, our destiny becomes cloudy and our inheritance feels stripped away. When we forget our identity, we will find fig leaves to cover up our freedom. This is the essence and heartbreak of shame.

Praise be to God, who broke the power of shame and set us free. He broke the chains of slavery, brought us out of Egypt, and has now lifted us up with Christ – far above the grip of shame and fear. Now, as we keep our eyes on Him, shame is but a distant foe.

"They looked to Him and were radiant, and their faces will never be ashamed." Psalm 34:5 (NASB)

Prayer: *Father, I thank You that I am not defined not by what I do, but who I am in You. Holy Spirit, I receive the power to walk as a confident child of God, free from shame and timidity. Strengthen me with might as I walk with You in the cool of the day. Amen!*

15

SEVEN ENEMIES OF DESTINY

"When the Lord your God brings you into the land where you are entering to possess it, and clears away many nations before you, the Hittites and the Girgashites and the Amorites and the Canaanites and the Perizzites and the Hivites and the Jebusites, seven nations greater and stronger than you, and when the Lord your God delivers them before you and you defeat them, then you shall utterly destroy them. You shall make no covenant with them and show no favor to them." Deuteronomy 7:1-2 (NASB)

When the Lord was calling Israel to conquer the promised land, He warned them of 7 specific enemies. Jews understand the significance of names and how they explain one's identity. These 7 people groups signify the enemies who war against who we are in Christ, and the meaning of their names can give us insight into their purposes, as they seek to drive back the people of God in their destiny.

The seven enemies of our destiny are: Fear, carnal living, accusation, discontentment, isolation, aimless living, and unrest. Although Jesus has conquered death and provided victory over these strongholds, we as believers still have to war against these fiery darts (and mindsets), in order to maintain our lot in this age. Whether it be fear or doubt, we must always be advancing with an awareness to defend and guard what has been given to us. Jesus warned that when the enemy is cast out, he will usually return seven times stronger (see Luke 11:24-26). Therefore, we must learn to occupy the territory He has set free.

1. HITTITE

    Hittite is the Hebrew word "chittiy" meaning, "fear, terror." Fear is probably the most utilized tool of the enemy—from it stems anxiety, stress, and paralyzing thoughts of doubt. This particular enemy was one who brought fear, terror, doubt, and ultimately confusion. If Israel came into agreement with this foul spirit, they would forfeit their courageous destiny.

    "The fear of man brings a snare, but he who trusts in the Lord will be exalted." Proverbs 29:25

    We war against this by understanding and receiving the Father's love. It is the great antidote for the fear of man. Nothing transforms the human heart more, than when God the Holy Spirit reveals God the Father's heart of love.

    "There is no fear in love. But perfect love drives out (conquers) fear, because fear has to do with punishment. The one who fears is not made perfect in love." 1 John 4:18 (**NIV**)

    Prayer: *Father, I thank You for Your perfect love. It is my defense in this life. Right now, I receive the strength to overcome fear as I come before Your throne in confidence, receiving grace in the time of need. In Jesus' name. Amen.*

2. GIRGASHITES

    Girgashites in the Hebrew language us "girgashiy" meaning, "dwelling on a clayey soil." Clay in the Bible represents the flesh (and our humanity). This group signifies the act of leaning on the flesh and depending on our own efforts. When the Lord cursed satan in the garden,

He told him, *"...And dust you will eat all the days of your life* (Genesis 3:14)." Dust in the Bible also signifies the flesh, and this reveals how the enemy feeds off the acts of the flesh. The enemy will constantly war with us in order to get us leaning on our own understanding and providence.

God has called us to be clay that is formed by Him. However, we must not lean on or trust in the clay alone. It is the Spirit in the clay that makes the difference. The ruach (breath of God) is the game-changer! Proverbs 3:5-8 in the Message Bible declares, *"Trust in the Lord completely, and do not rely on your own opinions. With all your heart rely on Him to guide you, and He will lead you in every decision you make. Become intimate with Him in whatever you do, and he will lead you wherever you go. Don't think for a moment that you know it all, for wisdom comes when you adore Him with undivided devotion and avoid everything that's wrong. Then you will find the healing refreshment your body and spirit long for."*

"For that man ought not to expect that he will receive anything from the Lord, being a double-minded man, unstable in all his ways." James 1:7-8

Being double-minded denotes the act of relying on two opposing mindsets at the same time. The Greek word "dipsychos" means, "wavering, uncertain, divided in interest." The enemy works to get us leaning on our flesh, thus dividing our focus and causing our hearts to waver.

We war against this with wholehearted devotion and focus on Christ. When we set our gaze on Jesus, our heart is calibrated to the place we were called to abide.

"Therefore, since we have so great a cloud of witnesses surrounding us, let us also lay aside every encumbrance and the sin which so easily entangles us, and let us run with endurance the race that is set before us, fixing our eyes on the author and perfecter of faith, who for the joy set before Him endured the

cross, despising the shame, and has sat down at the right hand of the throne of God." Hebrews 12:1-2 (NASB)

> **Prayer:** *Father, I commit my heart afresh to You. I give myself to righteousness and the Holy Spirit's work of sanctification. I declare that I am an instrument of righteousness, for Your glory. Amen.*

3. AMORITES

Amorites is the Hebrew word "emoriy" meaning, "sayer." The root word "amar" means "to command, to boast, to act proudly." This meaning is a double-edged sword. For example, the enemy uses words and accusations to stifle our confidence and bring confusion. They are his fiery darts. He will boast in his power to get us doubting. Accusing is what he does day and night; it is his full-time occupation (see Revelation 12:10).

We war against this by walking humbly before our God, by receiving and declaring the (written and spoken) word of God in our lives. His Word (not our own) becomes our boast. Isaiah connected the realms of humility and trembling before God's Word; they work hand-in-hand (see Isaiah 66:1-2). One of the keys given to Joshua to obtain the promise, was to cling to God's Word (see Joshua 1:8). In the time of Samuel, peace existed between Israel and the Amorites (see 1 Samuel 7:14). It was the prophetic (rhema) Word that drove back the intimidation of opposing armies of Israel. O, how we need the prophetic word restored to the church.

"But by a prophet the Lord brought Israel from Egypt, and by a prophet he was kept." Hosea 12:13 (NASB)

Later, it tells us that Solomon brought the enemies into slavery, by reigning over them entirely (see 1 Kings 9:20-21). Where Samuel represented revelation, Solomon represented wisdom. It takes the spirit of wisdom and revelation to subdue the voice of the enemy and live according to the voice of our Shepherd.

"When wisdom wins your heart and revelation breaks in, true pleasure enters your soul." Proverbs 2:10 (TPT)

> **Prayer:** *Father, I love Your Word. Sweeter than honey to my lips, it is life to my soul. I ask that You would stir a fresh hunger for Your (written and spoken) Word. In Jesus' name. Amen.*

4. CANAANITES

One translation renders the meaning, "merchants who humiliate." The Canaanites were financial giants, motivated by greed and lust for continual promotion and earthly gain. This giant opponent usually leads to unhealthy comparison and forsaking the uniqueness of who He made us to be.

Paul warred against this spirit in Athens, when he became greatly irritated by the ideology of Greek philosopher Epicurus, who taught that life was for personal pleasure and materialistic gain (see Acts 17:18). This idea grossly resists the heart of the gospel, of laying down our life for others.

"The world does not object to your being a Christian for a time, if she can but tempt you to cease your pilgrimage, and settle down to buy and sell with her in Vanity Fair." -Charles Spurgeon

We war against this with contentment and gratitude. I personally believe that one of the primary reasons Israel couldn't get out of their wilderness wandering was because of their discontentment. Numbers 11:1 says, *"Now the people became like those who complain of adversity in the hearing of the Lord."* In other words, the fabric of their attitude wouldn't allow destiny to flow. Rather, it stood as an obstruction to their promised land. This is why I believe that manifesting gratitude is one of the most courageous things a believer can do. It is the will of God!

"…in everything give thanks; for this is God's will for you in Christ Jesus." 1 Thessalonians 5:18 (NASB)

> **Prayer:** *Father, in thankfulness, I lift my hands and open up my heart. Holy Spirit, would you come and stir up a grateful attitude within me. In every season, may I constantly be in remembrance of Your goodness. In Jesus' name. Amen.*

5. PERIZZITES

This is the Hebrew word "perizziy" meaning, "belonging to a village." They were known as having their own isolated village, but with no walls or protection. The root word means, "open region." The enemy will seek to get us alone and isolated in an open region, so he can then attack and devour us. Remember, Scripture tells us that satan seeks *"like a lion,"* for lions will always go after the lone ranger, the easiest prey (see 1 Peter 5:8).

We war against this by living in community and fellowship with other believers. Jesus never promoted lone ranger ministry, rather He commanded His disciples to go out two by two (see Mark 6:7). Heaven's commander and chief wanted to bring a family dynamic to His ministry, and later we see that koinonia (fellowship) became one of the pillars of the early church (see Acts 2:42).

> **Prayer:** *Father, I thank You for the family of believers you have surrounded me with. I choose to lay aside any differences that would cause me to draw back, and I press in to fellowship, for the glory of Your name. Amen.*

6. HIVITES

This word renders the meaning, "villagers." They dwelt in tents, signifying their unrest and unsettled lifestyles. It speaks of wandering aimlessly and without purpose or vision. In the Arabic, one of the descriptions of this word is "to roll oneself in a circle which is altogether needless." When we fail to enter into rest and the finished work given by Jesus, we become wanderers living disconnected from the promised land.

"Where there is no revelation, people cast off restraint; but blessed is the one who heeds wisdom's instruction." Proverbs 29:18 (NIV)

"For this reason, since the day we heard about you, we have not stopped praying for you. We continually ask God to fill you with the knowledge of his will through all the wisdom and understanding that the Spirit gives, so that you may live a life worthy of the Lord and please him in every way: bearing fruit in every good work, growing in the knowledge of God, being strengthened with all power according to his glorious might so that you may have great endurance and patience, and giving joyful thanks to the Father, who has qualified you to share in the inheritance of his holy people in the kingdom of light." Colossians 1:9-12 (NIV)

The way we war against this is by embracing greatness. We were created to live exhilarated and filled with God-sized purpose – our destiny is packed with heavenly potential. Just as He told Abraham, so He leans over and urges us to dream and believe for greatness (see Genesis 12:2).

Prayer: *Father, I choose to see myself as a child of God, destined for greatness. I refuse any notion that would cause me to see myself as insignificant or invaluable. As a child of the King, I take up Your nature and press on in the greatness of God. Amen.*

7. JEBUSITES

Jebusite is the Hebrew word "yebuqciy" meaning, "a place trodden down." It signifies something that is beneath one's feet, and subdued by opposing forces. This was the purpose of the enemy in wilderness testings, to wear down and subdue God's Son – coming to Christ in His weakest (physical) moment. In the same sense, the enemy uses whatever means necessary to wear down the saints. In fact, one of the weapons of the antichrist (spirit) is the wearing down of the saints (see Daniel 7:25). It was once said, *"If satan can't make you bad, he'll make you busy."* -unknown

David was the one who would eventually conquer Jebus, by taking possession of Ornan, the Jebusite's threshing floor. It takes worshipers to overcome the "wearing out" of the enemy. Worship is that which silences the enemy and makes room for the rest of the Lord to settle in our hearts, making us immune to the enemies' devices.

"Worship stops the noise of life. Worship directs every fiber of our being heaven-ward." -Darlene Zschech

One of the interesting things about the Jebusites is that their worship included child sacrifice. Many saints are so worn down and exhausted that they make little to no time for legacy and the proceeding generation. Let us break off this spirit of "worn-out" and advance in the rest of the Lord.

Prayer: *Father, I awaken to my identity as a child of God. With worship as my warfare, I step into the rest that You give so freely. In Jesus' name. Amen.*

CONCLUSION

All of these enemies can be conquered by those who are fully submitted to His presence. It's not the smartest nor is it the best looking who defeat the enemies' plans. Beloved, conquering belongs to those who are consumed by the promises and presence of the Lord. Friends who desire His nearness are those who strike fear in the heart of their enemies. Remember Joshua, who finally conquered the promised land – he was the one found remaining in His presence.

"Inside the Tent of Meeting, the Lord would speak to Moses face to face, as one speaks to a friend. Afterward Moses would return to the camp, but the young man who assisted him, Joshua son of Nun, would remain behind in the Tent of Meeting." Exodus 33:11 (NLT)

May we never enter into covenant (agreement) with these foul enemies of our destiny. Rather, let us recognize and overcome the enemies of our promised land, taking ground for the Kingdom of our Lord Jesus Christ.

16

CULTIVATING OUR IDENTITY

Contrary to the old covenant, living under the new covenant now becomes about guarding what we already have (in Him). Paul says in Galatians 5:1, *"...keep standing firm and do not be subject again to a yoke of slavery."* The saints at Galatia had come out of (a spiritual) Egypt, and the apostle was urging them to guard their freedom in Christ. In other words, they would have to leave the place they were currently at to return to their former residence. Although our freedom can't be earned or lost, the expression of it can be weakened. This is why we must guard our place in Christ.

In the natural, when I guard something, it implies that I already have possession of it. If I build a fence around my house to keep intruders out, it is a sign that I want to protect my possession. The fence in no way implies that I am earning what lies behind it. Rather, it reveals my desire to keep what I already possess, untainted and untampered with. With that said, many times the Lord will only release through us what we are willing to protect.

GUARD WHAT WE HAVE

For whatever reasons, the word and topic of sin can often be neglected in the body of Christ. I understand (and support the idea) that we don't need to be "sin-conscious" and live in reactive mode. By all means, walking with a mind fixed on His presence is the better way. However, I do believe the lack of addressing sin, reveals a greater problem in our hearts. Let me explain…

I've never been to a doctor's appointment where the physician dances around the problems. Instead, if need be, they head straight for the issue at hand. It's their duty. They'll never spend the majority of time telling you how good your liver is when there is an obstruction in your kidney. They won't celebrate all the "positives" of your frame and send you home oblivious, if there is something hindering your body from operating at it's best capacity. Rather, it is their job to bring some of the "negatives" to the surface for the sake of removing them. This is a doctor's purpose in bringing your body to the fullest health.

> *"Later, Jesus and his disciples went to have a meal with Levi. Among the guests in Levi's home were many tax collectors and notable sinners sharing a meal with Jesus, for there were many kinds of people who followed him. But when the religious scholars and the Pharisees found out that Jesus was keeping company and dining with sinners and tax collectors, they were indignant. So they approached Jesus' disciples and said to them, Why is it that someone like Jesus defiles himself by eating with sinners and tax collectors? But when Jesus overheard their complaint, he said to them, "Who goes to the doctor for a cure? Those who are well or those who are sick? I have not come to call the 'righteous,' but to call those who are sinners and bring them to repentance."*
> Mark 2:15-17 (TPT)

PRACTICING OUR IDENTITY IN CHRIST

It takes intentional focus and diligence to grow in righteousness, peace, and joy. It doesn't come easy, but requires that we set our face on Him, and implement a few principles. Check out a few of the things I have done over the years, that have propelled me into greater dimensions of His love:

Be Holy: Holiness is the call to guard what we have been given. While the law says we must live holy to earn God's favor, holiness is actually the call to guard the favor we already have. If I owned a Lamborghini sports car, you better believe I would treat it with extreme care. It would be absurd for me to stand in my garage and wish I had a nice car that I could drive around on a sunny day. Anyone would say, "Robby, you have the car right in front of you. Now take that baby for a spin!"

Same goes with the gift of salvation in Christ – we already have the things necessary to live victorious in a broken world (see 2 Peter 1:3-4). All we need is faith to believe and the passion to guard what we already have. In other words, the sports car is in our possession, we must now get in the driver's seat and take it for a spin.

"Beloved, with promises like these, and because of our deepest respect and worship to God, we must remove everything from our lives that contaminates body and spirit, and continue to complete the development of holiness within us." 2 Corinthians 7:1 (TPT)

Did you see how Paul addresses the call of consecration? He says, *"with promises like these."* Another way to say it would be, "considering these promises…" or "in light of these promises." In other words, he is calling us to live up to the standard (and promise) of our calling in Christ. In the book of Ephesians, he calls us to live up to the reality of our high calling: *"Therefore I, a prisoner of the Lord, beg you to lead a life worthy of your calling, for you have been called by God* (Ephesians 4:1)." To "lead a life worthy" is to guard what we have.

In other words, those who are called to be kings and priests to God should act like it. If we are royalty, never should we live the lifestyle of a slave. If we are blessed with every spiritual blessing in the heavenly realms (see Ephesians 1:3), then why should we stoop to eat off the floor like a dog. We have been invited to eat from the King's table, and never should we be rummaging through the dumpster.

On the contrary, we must customize our lives to fit inside the reality of being in Christ – never allowing the outer to influence the inner. Rather, we must keep our hearts pure, allowing the light of the gospel to shine through our lives. If I were to hold a piece of black construction paper over the end a flashlight, the light beam would be obstructed. It wouldn't cease to be a light but the paper would definitely alter its natural function. The inherit design of that flashlight would need no obstruction to serve its full capacity.

In the same sense, our lives are to be a light and beam of hope to those around us. When we choose to dabble (or live) in sin, we are allowing obstructions to that light. By doing so, we don't cease to possess light, we just obstruct what is already there. A lighthouse lamp doesn't function beneath the water, rather it rests on top of the pedestal that all may see it when it's on. It sits nicely behind a glass to keep anyone and anything from being placed in front. In other words, the light is under guard.

Holiness therefore, is more of a call into one thing than it is a call out of something. Many treat repentance as a turning from, but often forget that it is as much a turning to. This is why all repentance and godly remorse must lead back to a surrendered life. Repentance that doesn't recalibrate our devotion to Jesus is not true repentance. It has to be a change of vision unto a greater change of heart. In fact, freedom in the gospel is a call unto a whole different realm of living and thinking. If we are set free and told to live the same as when we were in the flesh, then why would we need the gospel? Rather, Spirit-led living is a call to be unlike anyone else who is outside of grace. Think about it, He takes peasants and makes us priests, beggars and makes us kings. This is a big deal!

> *"True freedom is not doing as we please. It's being enabled to do the right thing well."*
> -Bill Johnson

Repentance: operating in the mind of Christ. The Kingdom of our Lord Jesus is totally opposed to earthly standards, and requires a different way of living and thinking. This is clear in Jesus' famous Sermon on the Mount, and explains why John the Baptist and Jesus both declared, *"Repent (change your thinking and perspective), for the Kingdom is at hand (within grasp)."* They understood for anyone to obtain the Kingdom of God, it would require a whole new mindset. Where the people were accustomed to seeing the Father and His dealings one (distorted) way, the new covenant would require a new perspective.

There are just some programs you can't run on your household computer unless there is first a processor change with frequent software upgrades. Same goes with us. We first receive a new heart (inward processor), and as we advance in our journey, it is imperative that we have frequent renewed perspectives (software upgrades). These changes allow us to steward what He is wanting to release in and through our lives.

Conformity into the image of Christ is the primary will of God, and as we shed the deeds of the flesh (disobedience, etc.) we manifest that will (see Romans 8:12-14). If you're like me, at one time or another you've heard your parents say, "act your age." This phrase is usually a response from the parent or authority who sees us living below the standard of our age. I have a sense that the Lord wants to address the church and say, "Church, act your identity."

> *"Since you have been raised to new life with Christ, set your sights on the realities of heaven, where Christ sits in the place of honor at God's right hand. Think about*

the things of heaven, not the things of earth." Colossians 3:2 (NLT)

Walk in Forgiveness: When we walk in the Spirit (by manifesting love, joy, peace, etc.), we are cooperating with the harmony of the Holy Spirit. Likewise, we must guard this precious harmony, by walking in forgiveness with our brothers and sisters. The Lord is orchestrating a global outpouring of His Spirit, and I firmly believe it will be sustained through maintaining "right relationships" in the body. If there is any breakdown of love in our midst, He will push "pause" on the manifestation, allowing time for healing and rebuilding. Friends, we cannot afford to go the way of offense. Instead, let us be diligent to keep the stream untainted and clean by honoring, forgiving, and loving one another.

A few years ago, the Lord gave me a real practical way to deal with offense. At the time, I was talking with a friend who was struggling with letting things go with a family member. In talking through it with him, I felt the Holy Spirit say, "Tell him he has 10 seconds to stay mad, and after that, he has to let it go." When I told him what I was hearing, he felt encouraged. You can bet that I began to apply that to my own life.

One of the problems with offense is, we get in one another's face with the issue, instead of God's. Rather than coming to the Lord with our hurts and pains, we sometimes go to others. This, my friend, can often create a bigger mess than we began with. I encourage you to go to the Lord with your hurts and pains. Let Him speak and bring healing and clarity to your brokenness. It's what He loves to do.

Prayer: *Father, I come before You. I know that You have called me to live free from offense. Right now in Your presence, I release (call out their name). I choose to let go of any hurts and disappointments that I have experienced. I receive Your mercy and extend it to them right now. Father, bless them and let Your face shine on them, in Jesus' name.*

Worship, worship, worship: one could define worship as beholding, and in my opinion, worship is the highest expression of beholding. They are one and the same. When we worship, we are turning our attention to the goodness and majesty of the Lord. As a plus, we become what we behold. When we gaze on the beauty of God, our soul is beautified with the same glory that Jesus walked in.

Jesus exemplified this perfectly, for when He did anything, it was from the place of beholding the Father. The Son of God didn't have a "ministry manual" He operated from, rather He simply followed the promptings of the Father. This required that He keep His heart and eyes fixed on the Father in heaven.

Devour the Word: it is so important to place high value on the Word. The Bible is our heavenly mirror, the spoken Word of God that presents us with images of our redeemed life in Christ. It shows us who He is, who we are, and what is available. In light of this, it gives us holy boundaries to keep us abiding in that reality. For example, the epistles encourage us in our identity as children of God, then urge us to live up to the standard of what He says about us. Thus, the Word of God is to keep us growing into mature children of God.

> *"Husbands, love your wives, as Christ loved the church and gave himself up for her, that he might sanctify her, having cleansed her by the washing of water with the word, so that he might present the church to himself in splendor, without spot or wrinkle or any such thing, that she might be holy and without blemish."* Ephesians 5:25 (NASB)

To drive home his point, Paul uses Old Testament references and language as a direct correlation to the tabernacle of Moses. When the priests were to enter the Holy Place, they were to wash their face and hands in an article called the brazen laver. Standing about waist-high to the priests, the laver was made out of the women's mirrors that had been melted down:

"Moreover, he made the laver of bronze with its base of bronze, from the mirrors of the serving women who served at the doorway of the tent of meeting (Exodus 38:8).*"*

The point of washing was to prepare them to experience the presence of God in the inner chambers.

In the same sense, giving ourselves to His Word is the most practical and powerful way to prepare our hearts for (experiencing and hosting) His presence. When we live devoted to the (written and spoken) Word of God, our hearts become more engaged with who He is and who we are in Him.

In Everything, Be Thankful: in Philippians, Paul gives a necessary ingredient to a life of prayer. He says, *"Be anxious for nothing, but in everything by prayer and supplication with thanksgiving, let your requests be made known to God* (Philippians 4:6).*"* Interestingly, Paul wrote this while he was imprisoned, suffering immensely for the gospel. How does one under such pressure, write *"be thankful in everything?"*

Thankfulness is like a broom that sweeps the mind from unnecessary clutter and junk. I always like to say, when you find yourself in a funk, just offer up thankfulness. If the walls seem to be coming in on you, push them back out with a heart of gratitude. Soon, the fog will lift and your heart will be calibrated to a place of praise.

I like to begin my personal prayer times with thankfulness. Most of the times it's being thankful for His goodness, demonstrated in His blood, the cross, and resurrection, but sometimes it's being grateful for waking up and enjoying another day. Either way, it's a way of acknowledging His existence in my life. If you're in the pit, be thankful. If you're on the mountain, be thankful. Whatever the case, just be thankful. It does miracles for the soul!

Find community: many speak of Paul, but very few mention Barnabas (whose name means "encourager"). Let me ask, where would Paul have been if he'd not had Barnabas by his side? Can you imagine the apostle without encouragement as a fellow companion? Another faithful companion in scripture was Nathan, a close friend of David – the prophet who spoke into David's life many times. The name "Nathan" means gift of God. Even though some of his interaction with the young king was confrontational, this prophet's friendship was a gift to David's life. His encouragement and admonishment were both beneficial and key in bringing David to a new level of thinking and seeking after God.

May we give ourselves to encouraging our fellow brothers and sisters in the Lord. Determine in your heart to be that Barnabas or Nathan in someone's life. Find that friend who you feel God has put in your life to provoke one another to higher heights. It's not only needed. Friends, it is necessary.

Renewing your mind: one of the clearest ways to demonstrate the will of God is by walking with a renewed mind (see Romans 12:1-2). Friends, how do we expect to bring renewal to the world around us, unless we first have a renewed mind? The upward call in Christ will always run in correspondence with minds that are set on His, and the way we think will set the trajectory of our lives.

Although walking in a renewed mind is glorious, it is a necessary discipline of the Christian walk. It takes intentionality and focus to give ourselves to the new man in Christ. Paul urged us to *"put on the new man* (see Ephesians 4:24."* Just like we would a jacket, putting on the new man requires us to reach into the Word of God and find what He has to say about us – even in the midst of circumstances and situations. With the myriad of options to think on, it is downright work to keep our mind fixed on things above. This process doesn't just happen, we definitely have to work at it. If it were easy, the whole world would do it. Instead, we have been called to a gospel that isn't always popular or held in the highest esteem. So, let us roll up our pant legs and jump into the rivers of right thinking – the dividends are glorious!

Get Rid of the Negative: when I say "negative," I am referring to that which steals our devotion and affection for Jesus. It is anything that takes our eyes off of Jesus. In many cases, it would apply to our thoughts.

It would be good to pray this right now; *"Father, in this moment, I align my mind with yours. I take up the Word of God and I war with the sword of the Spirit. I refuse to embrace any thought that is not in your mind. I renounce any ideas that destroy purity and power and at this moment, I give myself to You. I am Yours!"*

It would also be good to make a list of things that are necessary in life. Things like job, family, church are an absolute for most anyone. On that same list, write down those things that are distractions – both potential and absolute. Take your time when making the list. Ask the Holy Spirit for insight as to what is stealing your affection. He loves to dethrone anything that takes You away from fellowship with Him. When you invite Him in, He zealously enters. Holy Spirit loves habitation!

Concluding prayer: *Father, it is an honor being Your son/daughter. I am so grateful for the price that Your Son paid, so I could come into the household of Your goodness. I ask that You would continue to reveal the glory of who Christ is, while unveiling the riches of who I am in Him. Let the Spirit of wisdom and revelation rest on me, in Jesus' name. Amen!*

OTHER RESOURCES FROM ROBBY ATWOOD

ON EARTH PRAYER CD
Recorded live in KC, Robby prays amidst live music, for the increase of the knowledge of God, Identity, and much more. Also featured on this album is Corey Russell of IHOP-KC.
This album includes 7 tracks total

GROUNDED IN THE WORD WORKBOOK
This study guide entitled "Grounded In The Word" is part of the EQUIP Collection series from One27 House of Prayer. Enjoy a journey into The Word of God, becoming grounded in the love of Christ! This resource is helpful for new and mature believers alike!

IDENTITY IN CHRIST WORKBOOK
This study guide entitled "Identity In Christ" is part of the EQUIP Collection at One27 House of Prayer. This resource is designed to take the believer on a journey discovering God's love for us and finding our true identity in Him.

PRAYER THE GREAT JOURNEY

In this book, take a journey with Robby as he explains the struggles as well as the successes learned in the place of prayer. In its eight chapters, Robby reveals his own journey and keys that propelled him to discover the joys and delight in prayer.

PRAYER STUDY GUIDE

In this 6 chapter study, Robby breaks down some of the key components of prayer and living a life of dialogue with the Holy Spirit. With chapters focused on developing the secret place, to insight of how to gain New Covenant "prayer perspective," Robby uses practical keys and insight that will aid you in making prayer a daily lifestyle.

For additional information on the ministry and resources of Robby Atwood, visit **www.one27hop.com** or **www.robbyatwood.com**

ABOUT THE AUTHOR

Growing up in a God-fearing home, Robby received Jesus as His Lord and Savior at an early age. Not long after, he became involved in ministry as a musician in the local church. At the age of 17, Robby had a life-changing encounter with the Holy Spirit that would forever change his course. With this encounter came a renewed focus to pursue the Lord and the ministry He had been called to. For nearly 12 years, he faithfully served at a prominent local church as a worship and prayer leader. In 2006, Robby received a clear word to build the Lord a corporate resting place, the house of prayer.

Robby now directs One27 House of Prayer in Somerset, KY., a ministry devoted to building a culture of worship and prayer, with a growing emphasis on equipping, community, and missions. It is his longing to build the Lord a corporate dwelling place, and to see a generation equipped to love Jesus, doing His works in every sphere of society.

www.ingramcontent.com/pod-product-compliance
Lightning Source LLC
Chambersburg PA
CBHW070151100426
42743CB00013B/2881